Anchoring the Altar

Anchoring the Altar

CHRISTIANITY AND THE WORK OF ART

Mark Patrick Hederman

Published 2002 by
Veritas Publications
7/8 Lower Abbey Street
Dublin 1
Ireland

Email publications@veritas.ie
Website www.veritas.ie

ISBN 1 85390 599 2

A catalogue record for this book is available from the British Library.

Veritas books are printed on paper made from the wood pulp of
managed forests. For every tree felled, at least one tree is planted,
thereby renewing natural resources.

Cover design by Bill Bolger
Printed in the Republic of Ireland by Betaprint Ltd

Contents

CHAPTER ONE

Anchoring the Altar

CHRISTIANITY IS NOT a political party, a social system, a club, a union or a league. It is not founded on a concordat, a manifesto, a policy statement or a creed. There is no such thing as a national church. Any allegiance to some ethnic, political, social or cultural subgroup must be eliminated or attenuated to the point of being acknowledged as something secondary. Christianity is a way of life; life at its fullest. Like most lives lived to the full, this is achieved through love. Christianity makes available the love-life of the living God. Access to that life, its source in our world, is established and guaranteed through a certain kind of liturgy.

This book is, therefore, about worship. It is about making sure that when we do worship we are surrounding the right altar in the right way and using the correct forms of worship. Otherwise we are deluding ourselves. Otherwise we are omitting from our lives the most important primary relationship we are capable of accomplishing. Without genuine and immediate contact with the living God we are living only half a life. Christianity proposes, to anyone who wishes to avail of it, a form of worship which guarantees such contact on a daily basis.

Many people today suggest that Christianity, as a religion, has done more harm than good to the planet and to humanity.

They hold that the Judaeo-Christian tradition is responsible for the inhuman manner in which we have treated each other in the past and, more especially, for the irresponsible and greedy way we have treated planet earth. Some who exclude Judaism from this blanket condemnation, who even hold Christianity responsible for the crime against humanity of the holocaust in the last century, claim also that Christianity turned Judaism into a rape of the 'natural' world.

Much of what has happened during the two thousand year history of Christianity is open to such accusation. Crimes and horrors have been perpetrated by its members and in its name. However, the point of view being presented in this book is that in spite of the aberrant behaviour of many of Christianity's adherents the truth which it embodies and which is its direct source and origin is still the truth that can save us and save our world. And by 'save' I mean accomplish for us, in us, through us, the highest form of life possible to imagine, both now and in eternity.

Before Judaism, most religions were 'natural': they were both a worship of nature and a natural worship. Their basis was fear. Fear that fragile human beings, the least likely species to survive on the planet, would be thwarted, starved, suppressed, by the Power or 'powers' of Nature. Religion was a strategy devised to appease, seduce, captivate, harness, delude, distract, disarm the overriding thraldom of these gods of the natural world, on which human beings depended for the air they breathed, the food they ate, the water they drank, the crops they cultivated, the herds they kept, the prey they hunted, and the health that allowed them to undertake and enjoy all of the above.

Judaism was the first atheism. It cut the roots of that sacral connection with the earth which tied humankind into a slavery of service to greater and lesser gods. Judaism's fulmination against every form of idolatry was an attempt to free humanity from slavery to divinity at whatever level. Every time primitive human beings heard a clap of thunder or a flash of lightning they fell to the ground in terror. They imagined powerful gods behind each manifestation of elemental fury. They had gods of fire, of water, of earth and of air. It was the genius of Judaism which released them from such fealty. The Jewish religion was built from an experience of liberation. The 'Exodus' was the essential movement and foundational origin of the Jewish people and the Jewish religion. Textually it can be shown that the book of Genesis and the account of creation in the Hebrew Bible are based upon more ancient accounts of the Exodus that are more primitive and original.

The essential movement of this religion is to detach deity from the earth and place it in a realm beyond, which is untouchable, unreachable. The account of creation is intended to show that God created everything in heaven and on earth. In other words that everything in the world we inhabit is the same as ourselves, a created object, a thing. God is essentially 'other' than such created stuff. Primitive humanity thought there were descending orders of divinities that inhabited the heavens, the stars, for instance; that there were gods of the ocean and gods lurking in every bush and tree in the countryside. Judaism swept away all those deities and squarely determined the essential difference between the created world and the 'other' world where the glory of the Lord dwelt in inaccessible splendour.

God put human beings in charge of this universe as his representatives as his 'image and likeness'. This was not to give them licence to destroy or diminish the rest of creation but to ensure that they realised their own full potential and nobility as sons and daughters of God. They should be free from all inferiority complexes, calling no one or no thing 'master'.

Judaism also changed the relationship with the divinity into a relationship of love between equals. This monotheistic God was not a whimsical tyrant who slaughtered and punished at will. He had entered a covenant with his partners on earth and this was embodied in the Law. The great intuition of the Jews was that the Law in this sense was greater than God. That God was in fact subject to the law, which was what established the equality of all of us, including God. The law, the Torah, was that great invention of an omnipotent God which allowed Him to abdicate his sovereignty and allowed us to establish our independence. It was the mortising conduit, like a lock in a river or canal, which allowed two levels to align with each other. Later, the law became hardened into a barrier and had to be replaced by the flesh and blood of Jesus Christ who carried in his person the everabiding link between us.

The Jewish religion not only established a new relationship of responsible stewardship with nature and the created world, it also changed the relationship of each of us as human beings to each other. Each one of us became a unique infinity, in short, a God. We were all placed on that pedestal and became Gods by adoption, which means equality with God and with each other, because there is no greater or lesser in unique. It is like zero, it is unmatched and equal to itself.

Love your enemy, welcome the stranger, treat everyone as your equal; treat them as you would treat yourself. All this ran contrary to the 'natural' order where most tribes thought of themselves as the chosen people, the place where the world began, and every other tribe as lesser and less favoured by the Gods. All human evaluation was hierarchical. Such is the basis of most sacral religions, which for the most part, condoned human sacrifice and found aliens and strangers the least troublesome of these necessary propitiatory offerings. Better no religion at all, Judaism would proclaim, than a 'natural' religion that demands the sacrifice of the alien on the altar of the incumbent.

There is a tendency today, both in ecologically sensitive observers and anthropologists, to demonise the Judaeo-Christian religious insight as having led to the domination and destruction of the planet, and to idolise the aboriginal and indigenous religions of the world as having had more respect for nature. This is, like every heresy (which word comes from the Greek word meaning to select or to choose), an exaggeration of one half of the truth to the exclusion of the other half. Because truth is always complex and comprehensive, it contains the correct elements in both sides. Most primitive religions were indeed 'respectful' of nature but at what price? It was mostly a dehumanising fear that caused it. So, the step forward towards freedom, the Exodus from the slavery of Egypt, led by Moses and accomplished by the Jews, was essential and definitive. Humanity was different from that time forward. Now, I agree that they took it too far, that humanity abused this privilege, or rather certain dominant tribes of humanity overreached their mandate, and that with the gargantuan growth of technological power, this became, in the last few centuries, the technological rape of the planet. But that eventuality must not blind us to the truth which made this option possible. We could have used such freedom more beneficently, and could still do so, but the ultimate value is that freedom itself.

Let me take an example that is parallel and which shows something of the nuance which I am trying to establish. The infamous (Spanish) Inquisition, which has become the caricature of the Catholic Church at its very worst, and which no one could possibly defend and everyone should repudiate in the name of humanity, was actually begun for humanitarian reasons that are understandable. Its original intention was to prevent the horrific injustice of mob hysteria and lynch law which spread like a plague all over Europe. The fear of witchcraft and of 'sacral' religious powers of one kind or other produced a reign of terror whereby anyone even mentioned as a witch was mobbed and lynched without trial. People could further their careers, appropriate lands, wreak revenge and settle scores, by falsely accusing neighbours or enemies of being witches or wizards, and the unfortunate victims were cruelly tortured and murdered. It was to counteract such unsupervised lynch law that the Church introduced a tribunal which would give some objective recourse to those accused of heresy of whatever kind. The later aberrations and abominations of the 'inquisition' should not distort the fact that it was begun to offset an evil even greater than it later became in itself.

Now such arguments might seem somewhat academic if it were not for the fact that these realities still exist today. There are still tribes, peoples, nations who have not been liberated by the Judaeo-Christian cutting of the umbilical cord with the earth. They are still living in sub-human fear of some deity, some principality or power, which reduces them to trembling non-entities when they should be walking tall and taking their place as equals. One Nigerian leader of the recent past has said of his own country: 'Nigeria is the one true giant of Africa. Her peoples constitute nearly one half of the black people of the continent and two in five of all black people in the world. The resources concentrated within her borders would be the envy of most countries in Europe and the Americas, her landmass is huge, her climate largely benign. All this should have made her not only the most powerful country in the black world, but among the dozen most powerful nations on the globe.' This is the view of the former leader of the Biafran war of secession. He communicated his views to the then BBC correspondent covering that terrible war which Biafra lost. The then BBC correspondent, who was Frederick Forsythe, said he had rarely met a more gifted human being. He wrote a book about him called *Emeka*, which was his first name. Obviously Emeka's analysis of Nigerian failure to measure up to its potential includes both its crippling history and geography which were both fashioned by its colonial past; it also results from more recent bad government and corruption: 'Without organization a society is destined to seize up, choke and eventually die. A state where the services do not function, where the citizenry is not disciplined, where crime at every level runs unchecked, where leaders are not accountable to the led, and where justice is available to the highest bidder – such a state cannot inspire in others outside that confidence needed for leadership abroad.' But there is more than that, he thinks, and this is where his argument touches the need for the Judaeo-Christian revolution at the heart of every person's liberated humanity. Emeka sees himself as inheriting a religion of another kind: 'Being Black means having a certain concept of life, of which the major strain is of being close to nature. But this also has a concomitant weakness in lack of technology and fear of the supernatural. . . . The Black man's God is a God of retribution; awesome, unapproachable and merciless. The White man's God is a God of love, mercy and forgiveness . . . Faced with a strange mountain . . . the Black man turns his back on this terrifying monster, seeks out a calf from his miserable herd and begins the regular sacrifice to the god of the mountain. Very soon the mountain has become sacred and therefore impenetrable. For me, Black means in a word "disadvantaged". The moral and emotional fabric of Western Civilization is based on the concept that Black and inferior are synonymous.'[1]

So, what I am saying is not that Judaeo-Christianity has had a benign influence on planet earth. I am admitting that its influence has led to unspeakable crimes and inexcusable exploitation. However, I am maintaining that such aberrations were not necessary, were not 'Judaeo-Christian' in essence; they simply resulted from the dangerous freedom which these specific religions instituted. And I am defending that freedom and the Judaeo-Christian tradition for alone effecting such freedom in an otherwise irretrievably cowed and terror-stricken humanity.

It took several centuries for humankind to work out the mind-blowing extent of that freedom. In Christianity itself, it was the Council of Chalcedon (451 CE) which defined it most accurately. The key verb here was the Greek *Sozein*, meaning to save. The incredible awareness dawned on these Fathers of the Church that God came on earth not just to 'save' us from ourselves but, more importantly, to save us from God. The scope and extent of that freedom accomplished by Judaeo-Christianity has only become apparent in the last century where we developed it sufficiently to allow ourselves to destroy, if we wished to, the whole planet. This life, this freedom, willed for us by the living God, has put our life definitively, and ever so vulnerably, into our own hands.

The fact that we have used this freedom to become genocidal monsters, technological murderers, planetarian devastators, is certainly attributable to Judaism and Christianity, but only because these were the instruments of our liberation, the teachers of our autonomy, the mid-wives of our freedom. Nothing must prevent us from recognising the irreplaceable and incalculable value of that freedom. Judaism and Christianity snapped our chains; what we began to use our hands for after that liberation is a different story, is our responsibility.

We have to understand that Judaeo-Christian tradition properly if we are to judge it and if we are to live by it.

Anything less, as St Paul warns is:

> According to human tradition, according to the
> elemental spirits of the universe, and not according to
> Christ. (Col 2:8)

When dealing with Christianity as well as everything else we
must follow the precept: 'test everything; hold fast what is good'
(I Thess 5:21). And when we are separating the chaff from the
wheat we must be careful not to throw out customs and rituals
which were natural and yet can be adapted to the worship aligned
to our new found freedom. On the other hand we must be careful
not to erect false idols and worship these on a Christian altar.
Anyone who would seek to place the living God on the same altar
as their deposed idol without a change not only in the subject and
the object but also in the movement of religious fervour, says
Martin Buber, another great twentieth century Jewish
philosopher, is guilty of idolatry. Religions of sacral power are
sedentary, nationalistic, partisan, racist and earthbound. They can
never be substituted for the religion of Christianity. Nor can this
Christian way of life be used to bolster them.

The origin of Christianity is outside our world, beyond our
understanding, above and beyond our nature. It comes to us
through revelation. It is the living God who makes this presence
known and felt in our world as something that comes from
elsewhere, as a meteor might come to earth from outer space.
Except that both the meteor and outer space belong to our
natural world. Christianity is, therefore, a mystery religion. It is
founded on a mystery, transmitted through a mystery,
understood, in whatever way that is possible, as a mystery.

The milieu in which Christianity took form was one quite
familiar with mystery religions. The cults of Eleusis, Dionysus,
Attis, Isis, Mithras for example offered their devotees, their

initiates (*mystes*), salvation (*soteria*) by dispensing cosmic life through various sacramental actions which allowed for essential change through participation with the deity. These mystery religions comprised both cultic actions such as meals, fertility rites, baptisms, investitures and symbolic journeys, and they involved hidden teachings, an arcane secret tradition with regard to which the initiates took vows of silence. Such secret knowledge differentiated them from outsiders.

St Paul uses much of the terminology of a mystery religion when introducing his converts to the essence of Christianity. *Mysterion*, the mystery, is the eternal counsel (wisdom, *sophia*) hidden in God (Eph 3:9) before ever the world came to be (1 Cor 2:7) whose eventual manifestation will mean the end of this world (Eph 1:10). The apostolic mission is part of the unfolding of this mystery (Eph 3:2,9) and Paul himself as steward of the mystery must be acquainted with these secrets, the gift of a prophet being to penetrate the mysteries of God (1 Cor 2:10; 4:1) and become acquainted with all the mysteries. *Mysterion* (the hidden mystery) is connected with *Kerygma* (the proclaimed message) as the Father is manifested by the Son, who is an epistle (from the Greek *epi* + *stellein*, meaning 'to send') from God. The words used by Paul in at least one of his own epistles (II Cor 4:6) are still causing difficulties of interpretation, coming as they do after his description of the Christians of Corinth as in themselves a letter of Christ 'prepared by us, written not with ink but with the Spirit of the living God, not on tablets of stone but on human hearts' (II Cor 3:3). The verse in question uses the Greek words *photismos tes gnoseos tes doxes tou theou*, 'the true "gnosis" owed to an action of the divine light', and is translated in the new revised standard version: 'For it is the God who said, "Let light shine out of darkness," who has shone in our hearts to give the light of the knowledge of the glory of God in the face of Jesus Christ.' So, all knowledge of God is a mystery both in the way it is communicated and the way it is received. No human agency has proprietory claims, production control, or distribution rights in this regard. The way a mystery is handed on is itself a mystery.

Tradition in the early church was a fund of unwritten customs and mysteries making up the sacramental and religious life of the community (*ta agrapha tes ekklesesias mysteria*), necessary for understanding the truth of revelation and pointing to the mysterial character of Christian knowledge as a gnosis of God (*gnosis theou*) which is a gift conferred through such traditions.

Later, very much later, this oral tradition was written down and eventually hammered into dogmas and a credal formulas which became the *breviatum verbum* (the abridged version) as John Cassian[2] calls the Symbol of Antioch, making allusion to St Paul in Rom 9:27-28, who in turn is alluding to Isaiah 10:22. It was in the fourth century that the preferred rendering of the Greek term for mystery became 'Sacrament' which referred most especially to Baptism and the Eucharist.

Gnosticism became the first heresy with which Christianity had to contend, and from which it had to differentiate itself. It is understandable that every attempt was made at that time to rid the newly established mystery religion of all connection with, and all ambiguous terminology redolent of, the circumambient local cults which threatened to invade, dilute or dissipate the originality which Christianity incorporated into its liturgy and sacraments. However, the bitterness and intensity of the struggle between Gnosticism and early Christianity was owing to their proximity rather than their difference; was caused by the similarity which threatened to absorb, rather than any heterogeneity which might define them as contradictory opposites.

Whatever the dangers of misinterpretation or of identification with alien religions, Christianity remains essentially a mystery religion. And this means that its substance, its secret core, can never become comprehensively enshrined in any work of human hands of whatever variety or intricacy.

Christ came on earth to reveal the mystery of that life which is lived eternally by the three persons of the Trinity. He replaced one mystery with another mystery. The only reality as mysterious as the three persons in one God is the reality of the human person. And this is the basis of our religion, the mystery on which it is founded. When Pilate asked Jesus, 'What is truth?' the answer was silence. The truth, in person, was standing in front of him. No more accurate or comprehensive embodiment of truth could have been present to him. The person is the only reliable expression of truth. Jesus Christ never wrote anything down himself. The only recorded account of his writing was with his finger in the sand in front of the woman taken in adultery. So, any account of his life or his teaching is second-hand. And all such accounts display glaring inconsistencies and irreconcilable disagreements.

The resurrection of Jesus Christ, which is the essential mystery upon which any faith in Christianity is based, was an unwitnessed event. No human person was present. Witnesses have testified to having seen his empty tomb; others claim to have met Jesus Christ in his resurrected humanity; but no one knows how or when his dead body was brought back to life.

Tradition for Christianity is the process whereby the mystery of Jesus Christ, the revelation of God's love in person, is transmitted by his followers. These followers are now organised into an official body called the Church. However, the truth which they transmit is ultimately derived from an oral preaching by the original bearers of this truth (which is no more and no less than privileged contact with Jesus Christ as the Risen Lord in person) passed on in many different ways through the ever-present agency of the Holy Spirit.

The word 'tradition' comes from the Latin for handing on, or handing over. In Greek the word is *'paradosis'* which is used in the New Testament both for the way in which Judas 'handed over' Jesus as betrayal in the garden (Mark 14:10; 1 Cor, 11:23) and the way Christians 'handed down' their beliefs (1 Cor, 15:3; 2 Thess, 2:14).

Every form and variety of tradition must travel the narrow path between these two translations. At every moment we can be betraying the truth and preventing people from seeing it. Tradition itself is free of every determination and cannot be contained in any formula, locality, or cultural manifestation; any historical embodiment limits it. Tradition in itself is silence and every word of revelation has a margin of silence. Certain nuggets hewn from this great silence have come down to us in both the Scriptures and Liturgical tradition but, as Ignatius of Antioch says (Ephesians 15:2), 'The person who possesses in truth the word of Jesus can hear also its silence'. If all the great silence of tradition had become scripture, St John tells us, 'then the world itself would not be able to contain the books that would have to be written'(John 21:25). The silence is our turning towards the great abyss of divine love, towards which every scrap of revelation, every detail of tradition, points.

Tradition as silence and as incomprehensible mystery translates itself into various traditions which help us to gain access to it. These can be found in certain human organisations, structures, documents, dogmas, formulae, creeds, etc. They can materialise through Councils of the Church, writings of theologians and doctors of the church, canonical prescriptions, liturgical practices, devotional practices, iconography, and so on. But they are all secondary tributaries of the original silence of Tradition, which remains unwritten and mysterious. Tradition as such can never be found in itself in the horizontal tapestry of local and cultural traditions. In fact, Tradition is the way in which the Holy Spirit allows each one of the faithful to detect the mystery of Christianity within the length and the breadth of the 'horizontal' pattern of traditions. St Paul prays for the Ephesians (Eph 3:18) that they may be able to 'comprehend with all the saints' not only what has become the 'length and the breadth' of Revelation but also its 'height and depth' which are never captured in the earthly forms.

Tradition from our point of view is more the unique way in which each of us is prompted to receive the 'words' of either scripture or liturgy, the symbols or the images of our cultural traditions, than it is any of those particulars in themselves. Ignatius of Antioch tells the Magnesians (8:2): 'It is not the content of the Revelation but the light that reveals it; it is not the word but the living breath which makes the words heard at the same time as the silence from which it came'. In this sense, tradition becomes more the Holy Spirit's gift of discernment to each of us, so that 'those who have ears to hear with, may hear what the Spirit is saying to the churches'. Tradition is no more or no less than the life of the Holy Spirit in the church communicating to each one of us as persons, bestowing on us the faculty of hearing, of receiving, of knowing the Truth in the light which is divine. This is the knowledge of the truth that will make us free.

In his novel, *The Brothers Karamazov*, Dostoevsky shows us in 'The Grand Inquisitor' some of the great temptations which beset every human being as a religious person. The story imagines that Jesus Christ returns to earth in Seville, Spain, in the sixteenth century and is personally confronted by the leader of the Spanish Inquisition. The Grand Inquisitor explains why Christ is so unwelcome back here on earth and why on the next day he is going to have him burnt at the stake as a heretic. His harangue is long-winded and intelligent. But as in former circumstances the Christ figure remains silent.

> "People, so long as they remain free, have no more constant and agonising anxiety than to find as quickly as possible someone to worship. But they seek to worship only what is incontestable, so incontestable, indeed, that all human beings at once agree to worship it all together . . . the absolutely essential thing is that they should do so *all together.* It is this need for *universal* worship that is the chief torment of every person individually and of humankind as a whole from the beginning of time."[3]

....

> "You knew, you couldn't help knowing this fundamental mystery of human nature, but you rejected the only absolute banner, which was offered to you, to make all people worship you alone incontestably – the banner of earthly bread, which you rejected in the name of freedom and the bread from heaven. And look what you have done further – and all again in the name of freedom! I tell you human beings have no more agonising anxiety than to find someone to whom they can hand over with all speed the gift of freedom with which the unhappy creature is born . . . For the mystery of human life is not only in living, but in knowing why one lives . . . And instead of firm foundations for appeasing our conscience once and for all, you chose everything that was exceptional, enigmatic, and vague, you chose everything that was beyond our strength, acting consequently as though you did not love us at all .

. . Instead of taking possession of our freedom you multiplied it and burdened the spiritual kingdom of human beings with its sufferings for ever. You wanted our free love so that we should follow you freely, fascinated and captivated by you. Instead of the strict ancient law, we were in future to decide for ourselves with a free heart what is good and what is evil, having only your image before us for guidance. . . . It was you yourself, therefore, who laid the foundation for the destruction of your kingdom and you ought not to blame anyone else for it. So . . . we have corrected your great work and have based it on miracle, mystery and authority. And people rejoiced that they were once more led like sheep and that the terrible gift which had brought them so much suffering had at last been lifted from their hearts. Were we right in doing and teaching this? Tell me. Did we not love humanity when we admitted so humbly its impotence and lovingly lightened its burden and allowed that weak nature even to sin, so long as it was with our permission?"

....

'When the Inquisitor finished speaking, he waited for some time for the Prisoner's reply. His silence distressed him. He saw that the Prisoner had been listening intently to him all the time, looking gently into his face and evidently not wishing to say anything in reply. The old man would have liked him to say something, however bitter and terrible. But he suddenly approached the old man and kissed him gently on his bloodless aged lips. That was all his answer. The old man gave a start. There was an imperceptible movement at the corners of his mouth; he went to the door, opened it and said to him: "Go, and come no more – don't come at all – never, never!" The Prisoner went away.'

'And the old man?'

'The kiss glows in his heart, but the old man sticks to his idea.'[4]

What Dostoevsky is so graphically describing is not just the church's inclination towards totalitarian authority, but, more importantly, our conniving penchant for such authoritarian rigidity also. Whether we are aware of it or not, everyone loves to have a strict governing authority somewhere in the background. And, indeed, as far as the church is concerned, there has to be one. Someone has to be responsible for saying yes or no on various questions and in difficult situations and this has to be one person, in the idiom of Christianity, the person with that particular charism and gift of discernment. The buck has to stop somewhere, as we all seem to agree everywhere, even today! The bishop is meant to be that person in each constituent diocese of Christianity. But even, and perhaps especially, among bishops there has to be one head. It is quite clear, from even a cursory glance at the New Testament, that Peter is *primus inter pares* (first among equals), even if it is also clear that he was by no means the most intelligent, the most sensitive, the most diplomatic, the most talented of the apostles. However, the way in which such priority and such leadership should be exercised is open to interpretation. Above all it must be a primacy of service.

We are perhaps fortunate over the last quarter of a century to have had a Pope who is so willing to be one. Someone who gets up every day for twenty-five years and is ready, willing, and able to be everyone's shadow daddy. And anyone with any spirit of fairness will have to admit that he has done it with panache.

Margaret Thatcher only lasted half that time. Ian Paisley is probably the only politician in Ireland who has been with us and shouting at us for as long.

Irish people too, in the meantime, have grown up and are not quite as biddable as they used to be, not quite as overshadowed by the father archetype. Despite all the papal ranting about contraception the school-going population is decreasing by eight thousand every year, nationally. These are facts not entirely owing to the rhythm method, which Pope Paul VI thought compatible with Catholic practice. Contraception for most Catholics these days is not one of the articles of the Creed. Even our older nursery rhymes have adapted their endings:

> There was an old woman
> Who lived in a shoe
> She didn't have any children
> She knew what to do!

Christianity is a living tradition. Its fundamental source is the Spirit who breathes where the Spirit will and who is independent of any ecclesiastical forms or formulae. These remain close to the Spirit as long as they are not removed from such contact. Liturgy and the original oral accounts of what happened were always seen as *Prima Theologia*, whereas dogma and the credal formulae which synopsised these and turned them into propositions were understood as *Secunda Theologia*. However, in recent years this comes as a surprise to most people. Alfred North Whitehead has put it starkly: 'Religions commit suicide when they find their inspiration in dogma'. And Vladimir Lossky, the great Orthodox theologian, says that 'a doctrine is traitor to tradition when it seeks to take its place'. Dogmas are a safeguard not a source. The word comes from the Greek for 'what seems right'. In essence Dogma proclaims that *Prima Theologia*, the primary text, can mean this and this, but not that. They put a fence around the meaning to safeguard it from corruption, dilution, oblivion.

Gadamer in his book *Truth and Method* makes a very interesting point: 'The general nature of tradition is such that only the part of the past that is not past offers the possibility of historical knowledge'.[5] The only way we can remember anything is through something which still exists in our contemporary world. There has to be some relic, memorabilia, remnant or historic remains that are still with us today and that allow us to determine the source of our historical knowledge, practice or belief. Nothing remains of the founding fact of Christianity except the effect it had on the contaminated survivors. How then does the tradition of Christianity survive? What is it that we remember?

'Do this in memory of me.' Christ is remembered after two thousand years in a series of cultic actions which are known to the faithful as the Liturgy of the Eucharist or more popularly as the Mass. How is this possible? If any one of us wanted to be remembered for even a hundred years what would we have to do? Football fans in the middle of the last century swore they would never forget the eight members of Matt Busby's Manchester United team who died in an air crash in Munich in February 1958. They would remember especially the star of the team, Duncan Edwards, who was twenty-one when he died. A former England team manager called Duncan Edwards 'the very spirit of British football'; at Old Trafford 'the supporters used to watch him in a state of perpetual adoration'. In Dudley cemetery his grave has a headstone with an ingrained picture of him throwing in the ball. One of the flower stands is a mock football. His father was a gardener at the cemetery. Visitors would say the same thing: there will never be another Duncan and we will never forget him. There is a stained glass window memorial to Edwards in his football togs in the parish church at Dudley. Mr and Mrs Edwards had two carrier bags full of letters of sympathy which came to them after Duncan died. Friday was a popular day for visitors to the graveyard, a lot of lorry drivers from Manchester among them, on their way home for the weekend and the match at Old Trafford. It is not yet fifty years since his death. How many still remember?

Cinema goers in the 1930s said that no one would ever forget the 'Queen of Comedy', Carole Lombard. She was married to the 'King', Clark Gable. She danced with George Raft in *Bolero*, played opposite William Powell in *My Man Godfrey,* and Charles Laughton in *They Knew What They Wanted,* directed Alfred Hitchcock himself in one scene of *Mr and Mrs Smith* and starred in Lubitsch's *To Be Or Not To Be,* before she died in a plane crash at Table Rock mountain close to Las Vegas on January 16, 1942 at the age of thirty-three.

Even Shakespeare, who is remembered through his plays and his poetry after four hundred years, has to be converted into cinema to reach a larger audience. Otherwise you have to be able to understand English to remember him; you have to be able to read. There are more illiterate people in the world today than there ever have been since the world began. None of these can participate in such acts of remembrance.

It is true that Aristotle, Plato, Euripides, Alexander the Great, among others, are remembered as household names in Western European civilisation. However, the exact content and the everyday effect of that reminiscence is minimal except in the case of a handful of professors and students.

Napoleon writing from exile on the island of St Helena tells his correspondent quite frankly that he is the greatest person who has ever existed on this planet. The reason for this, he explains, is that by the sheer force of his personality, by his real physical presence, he could get any person standing in front of him to do whatever he wanted them to do. His point is well illustrated by the hundred days after his return from that exile when the whole of France seemed to capitulate to his sheer presence and allowed him once again to take charge. However, even he makes one exception. There is one other person who is greater than he and this person is Jesus Christ. And the reason why he is greater, Napoleon tells us, is that he can exercise such magnetism over people thousands of years after he was physically on earth. His personal presence is not reducible to, nor dependent upon, his physical historical reality as a human being.

Shelley has a wonderful sonnet, 'Ozymandias', which, according to Diodorus Siculus, Greek historian of the first century BC, was the Greek name for Ramases II, who reigned in Egypt thirteen centuries before Christ was born. Ramases wanted to be remembered forever and so had erected the largest statue ever seen in Egypt with the inscription: 'My name is Ozymandias, King of Kings,/Look on my Works ye Mighty and despair!' He meant to imply that anyone looking at this statue would despair of ever being in any way important in comparison with him. However, the words now read with mocking irony because the statue has long since been destroyed.

> Nothing beside remains. Round the decay
> Of that colossal wreck, boundless and bare
> The lone and level sands stretch far away.

And yet, two thousand years after he did it, Christ's act of remembrance is still performed all over the world. And, again, we must be clear that this is performance art. It is not enough to think about it, or to commune with it in the Spirit. It is an act, a deed, and it has to be done.

All of which helps to show that the way in which Jesus Christ is remembered after two thousand years is so ingenious that anyone can avail of it, anyone can participate. You don't have to be able to read; you don't have to belong to any tribe or tongue. You can be there at the mystery whoever you are.

That is why it is a rite, a cult. Doing 'this' means an action, something done. It is not something written, something promulgated, something explained. It is the mystery unfolded in our presence.

Which means that Christ was also the greatest artist the world has ever known. He left behind him a work of art which endures after two thousand years. It was a very simple and direct act. But as a work of art it was a five sense breakthrough to the world of humanity. In fact we can even make a parallel between the five wounds of Christ and that five sense breakthrough in the liturgy. The wounds were the breakthrough in the other direction towards God. The Latin word for such wounds (*vulnera*) is the same as our word for vulnerability. God made himself vulnerable to us. We had a way through to him. This is what we mean by transcendence: a way out of our human situation to a beyond. In theology there were always four ways to make this breakthrough. These were called the transcendentals: they were, and are, The Truth, The Good, The One, and The Beautiful. In the past the first three were emphasised – we had the truth presented to us in creeds and formulae of faith, or we stressed the good in terms of ethics and precepts of morality, or we aimed towards unity either in marriage or in ecumenical effort. Today it is the fourth of these ways towards transcendence which seems to be the more accessible and appropriate.

In the Catholic Church one of the greatest theologians of the twentieth century, Hans Urs von Balthasar, built his life's work on the beautiful as the icon of our lives. However, any of these paths towards transcendence, towards relationship with God, are equivalently valid. It does not matter which station you take to enter the subway, as long as you reach the same track that serves each one as a means of transport. As the great artist of the Fourth Gospel puts it (John 14: 2-4):

> There are many rooms in my father's house;
> if there were not, I should not have told you.
> I am going now to prepare a place for you,
> and after I have gone and prepared you a place,
> I shall return to take you with me;
> so that where I am
> you may be too.
> You know the way to the place where I am going.

Anchoring the altar requires four kinds of presence, at all times of change, development or inculturation: the priest on one side of the altar with the people on the other. Whether the priest faces in any particular direction, whether the priest is a man or a woman, whether the priest is married, celibate or in a relationship with someone, all of these are secondary and optional. The important fact is that whoever is celebrating the Eucharist should be an ordained minister. The ordination ceremony is one of the most significant examples of Tradition as silence. The moment of transmission of the ministry of priesthood takes place during a rite in which the bishop and other ordained ministers who are present place their hands in silence on the head of the one to be ordained. Tradition as the power of the Holy Spirit conferred upon the newly ordained happens as this silence.

Apart from the priest on one side of this altar, the people are, of course, the essential ingredient at the other side. So much has been written and spoken in a condescending attempt to make people take themselves seriously! There is no church, no incarnation, no resurrection, no creation, no love, no sacraments, no mystery, without people. In the liturgical space every single person is infinite, eternal, total, and complete. Uniqueness allows for no comparisons, no hierarchies. Around the altar each one of us, and this includes the persons of the Trinity, are unmatched, peerless, and nonpareil, and each one of us is equal to the other. Any perceived disparity of either distinction or importance is of the order of service, a job that has to be done, for which someone is chosen or appointed. There are different charisms and different gifts, but the essential core of personhood is both what matters and what constitutes each of us as distinctive and each of us as loved.

So, again in this realm of charism, just as in the icon (whether written or painted) of the Transfiguration, while the chosen disciples were worshipping on the mountain, to the left and right of Christ transfigured, there were two other representative figures: Moses and Elijah. So too the Church transfigured today requires two other charisms and 'gifted' persons to give balance and beauty to tradition renewed. These two are the anchorite and the artist.

The word anchorite means hermit or recluse. It comes from the same root word for place, *chora*, which the Greeks reserved for that second kind of space which is opening to a sacred dimension. This person has to be in living contact with the risen Lord, a contemplative who has direct access to the Holy Spirit, a medium of tradition because rooted in its source. Such a person is in this world but not of this world because energised by the time-space dimensions of resurrected life. In this dimension there is neither male nor female and it is unimportant which gender happens to grace any particular moment or occasion, but spiritual history attests, right from the first historical manifestations of resurrected life, that women are more likely to be in place.

Artists are the last on the list of required attendants at this liturgy although there is no hierarchical or ranking order involved. The reason I place them last in this account is because I have already tried to describe their essential role in depth and in detail in a previous book.[6]

Other ways of enumerating the four square posters which should anchor the twenty-first century altar would be: the priest, the prophet, the poet and the practitioners. When each is pulling their weight the altar is secure in the middle.

The Christian Church is built on the foundation of the apostles and the prophets. The apostles were those chosen by Christ to report him and his cause aright to the unsatisfied. They had privileged contact with the risen Lord and with the person of Jesus as an historical human being. However, their particular charism did not emerge until after his death and resurrection and until the descent of the Spirit at Pentecost, specifically named – Pentecost referring to the fiftieth day – (during which time the so-called 'apostles' were cowering in an inner room terrified of their lives to come out!) to emphasise the gap between the physical departure of Jesus from this earth and the arrival of the Holy Spirit. So, something happened to them which was the foundation of the Church and it did not happen to them while Christ was with them, it happened fifty days after he had left them and it changed them into apostles, people with a mission. The last of these apostles was St Paul. He wasn't present at all during the lifetime of Jesus and yet he had his resurrection experience on the road to Damascus long after the other apostles. So, the essential point is this: the foundation of the Church is not attached to any historical moment in time and is not directly linked to the life of Jesus Christ as an historical personage of Jewish origin living in Palestine two thousand years ago. The foundation of the church is a mysterious connection between the risen Lord and individual persons who experience his resurrected person as an event which also causes them to participate in his resurrected being and transforms each one into an apostle.

The Catholic Church has in the past tried to locate this foundation in a particular place at a particular time. It has sought to limit the energetic connection between the risen Lord and his apostles to the group of twelve who were his disciples. However, even the anomaly of St Paul, who must be given much of the credit for the effective spread of the Gospel in early times, defeats that proposition. Apostles did not have to be alive at the same time as Jesus. Transmission of this charism can occur any time anywhere.

The next attempt to limit the ubiquity of foundational power in the risen Christ was the notion of horizontal and unbroken transmission of the charism from the first apostles to the present day. Thus, the hands on transmission of the episcopal office from pope to pope and from bishop to bishop, which of course meant that any break in the chain or any deviant assumption of the episcopal office destroyed the link, cut off the power and rendered impotent all those dependent upon such sources for their ordination to the apostolic role. Any objective study of popes and bishops since the original ordinations supposedly carried out by Christ himself must give the lie to any such theory of unbroken, uncontaminated, continuous apostolic succession. Certainly at one point in Church history there were three popes alive and claiming such unbroken succession. The Holy Spirit at that time did not decide that they were two too many but rather three too many and as usual the Spirit blew where the Spirit willed to establish or re-establish apostolicity.

The original monks in the church were almost obsessed by the notion of establishing the apostolic roots of monastic life. Founders of monasteries, like John Cassian, went to endless trouble to establish that at least one of the apostles had been there to start their movement. Similar mythologies brought Andrew to Russia and to Scotland, for instance, Thomas to India and Mary Magdalene to Marseilles. Whether any or all of these ever did undertake such journeys is doubtful. The point was that unless the monks or the church in a particular area could claim that one such personage had been present when they set up shop it was not possible to ratify what they were doing and establish the credentials of their way of life as a legitimate continuation of the life which God had sent Jesus Christ to establish on earth.

The Church in Ireland was hard put to establish its pedigree and counter accusations of illegitimacy. St Patrick was swiftly elevated to the rank of apostle – the apostle of Ireland – and portions of his Confessions agonise over the possibility of his not having been officially and legitimately mandated by Rome.

Now, the truth of the matter is that unless the church anywhere is founded on the living connection between at least one 'anchorite' and the living God, it is in danger of apostasy. Apostolic foundation and succession is dependent upon living connection in the here and now between at least one person in the church and the living God. 'When I return will I find faith upon earth' is a moment by moment concern of the three persons of the Trinity. And they are not going to find this in churches, curiae, tabernacles or ciboria, they will find it only in living persons. The church is founded on the apostles and the prophets and not on any stone or document or legal formula or dogmatic treatise or official catechism or established ritual. And this means that unless it is anchored in the relationship between the risen Christ as a person and the person of some either apostle or prophet who has been graced by the Holy Spirit with a real live personal connection with that risen Christ, which is the reality of resurrection, and which allows them to say with utter conviction that Jesus is Lord and that God is Father, then there is no guaranteed church in that place. All the secondary tributaries of the river of life, whether they be institutional, pedagogical, liturgical, structural, socio-economic or political are directly and unequivocally dependent upon personal connection with the source. And that source is nothing more or less than at least one person's real relationship with the living God.

After that hypostatic union, to use a technical term, the rest can follow. But that is why it is essential to anchor the altar in the only source of its meaning and power, its efficacy and its orthodoxy, which is the unbroken and distinctly personal life of prayer – meaning by prayer person to person contact with the living God. The mystery of what happens on and around the altar, which is so vitally important to the authentic life of any community, is the mystery of connection between the person of Jesus Christ, his real presence, and the person or persons of those who surround that altar. Remove that connection and any or all liturgy is dead. It is an empty tomb without the risen body and blood of the man Jesus. And that resurrection is a dynamic communion between the risen lord and those around the altar who have also risen from the dead through direct communion with his risen presence. Ultimately the anchor is personal faith.

When we say that Christianity uprooted all 'natural' religion from its earthbound, sacral, umbilical connection, we are not saying that it thereby dismissed or discarded every cultural attempt to worship the living God. Once the basic fuse has been changed and once the worshipping community is effectively plugged into the genuine source of life, then every manifestation of local, indigenous, historical, cultic and cultural gestures, postures, rituals and rites of worship can be and should be harnessed and appropriated.

Catholic imagination, especially in its Celtic version, is sacramental. For it, all natural reality is 'sacramental' which means, as Andrew Greeley has taken great pains to establish from a sociological point of view,[7] that it is a revelation of the presence of God.

Greeley's book is important because what he is trying to do is bring together in dialogue at least three areas of life which have been ignoring each other for one whole century: the areas of art, science and religion. And he is able to do this because he happens to be a priest, a social scientist and a novelist himself. He writes like a storyteller and the advantage of his book is his capacity, which is a rare one, to make perfectly clear and transparent what is in his own mind and what he is trying to get across to the reader. So, it is possible for anyone, who is interested, to read the book. You don't have to be a theologian, an artist, or a scientist to follow his argument. He has a refreshingly brash disrespect for academic boundaries, esoteric enclaves and scholarly or philosophical subtlespeak. Nothing is off-limits in his argument and no holds are barred. He can tell you, in one page for each, what Marx, Freud, Durkheim, Malinowski, Simmel, Max Weber, Talcott Parsons (and by extension Clifford Geertz) Rudolf Otto, William James, and Mircea Eliade have to say about religion, in case you feel shy about joining the discussion. And then he makes his own argument crystal clear: Religion is alive and well in our world. Those who say that it is dying or dead, that 'secularisation' has taken over, are imposing their own 'dogmas' on an unsuspecting and, maybe, willing public. The 'facts' are clear: most of us are religious and can't help being religious. It's like our sweat, it comes with the body: they go as a set. Being human means being 'religious', otherwise we die of depression or despair. Life is the first disease. Death is the second, which forces us to hope. Religion is the way we deal with these three. And 'religion' is not propositional, not a creed, to start out with.

It is a story. The story is the virus which harbours and spreads the dis-ease which everyone is bound to catch because most of us are born into a family or bear a family of our own; and family is where we become inevitably infected with a particular brand of religion. And of course we can deny this or repudiate it later on. But the overwhelming evidence suggests that 'people' today are as 'religious' as ever and are likely to remain so. And to be planning a new world for such people without taking this factor into account, is foolhardy.

His panoramic sketch of religiosity in the Middle Ages undergirds his theory that the world was never really 'Christian' and that Christianity never exercised the cultural hegemony that many take for granted.

Whether his argument is founded or not, I am taking it as a basis for discussion. It is possible that 'religion' is a natural phenomenon that locks us into a particular culture, especially when it is 'the storytelling community' which 'develops its own methods for determining which versions of a story are acceptable and which are not'.[8] However, my contention is that Christianity and Judaism were and should be freeing us from the bonds of slavery to any religion which would be tribalistic and demand as its prerequisite either the scourging or the crucifixion of its members as is the reported case in New Mexico or the Phillipine Islands. Even though Christianity can adopt many of the endearing, colourful and creative aspects of any such sects, it must always remain an *agent provocateur* rather than a preserver of the necrophiliac instinct of any such religion. The story of Christianity and of Judaism is the story of the Exodus, the passover from crippling culture into resurrected freedom. Any version of either that confirmed and established a religion of fear or of punishment would be betrayal.

Sociologically I agree wholeheartedly with this author, we must take seriously the religious factor, but theologically we must ensure that nothing (neither story, nor poem, nor ritual, nor religion) can separate us from the love of Christ.

In his later book *The Catholic Imagination*, Greeley shows another even more important aspect of living religious tradition. He shows that this reality exists even in what academics call post-Christian society. The way such imagination is passed on is not by the channels of official church teaching or catechetical instruction, it is imbibed from the breast of storytelling incubators where each of us were children and adolescents watching and listening to what was being conveyed to us through our living environments.

Alongside a puritanical and dogmatic diet of condemnation and censure of all eroticism in our religion and personal behaviour, there was and is always another tradition, an artistic tradition which dared to display, and so much more transparently and effectively, the essentially erotic nature of our lives and our religion and, indeed, the erotic nature of divine love. Anyone who has viewed Bernini's statue of St Teresa in divine ecstasy will know that the artist presents her in an orgasmic state. The statue is beautifully reproduced on the cover of Greeley's book for those who have not had or may never have the opportunity of viewing the original. Anyone who has attended the Easter vigil and watched the candle being plunged into the water and heard the Latin prayer that accompanies the rite will know that we are representing the passionate union between Christ and the Church as the sexual union of a man and a woman, which from the book of Genesis is the chosen image for the way we are made in the image of God. Anyone who reads the Song of Songs in the Bible or the poetry of John of the Cross is left in no doubt about the erotic passion of real relationship with God. All marital liturgies are full of comparisons between the love of the bridegroom and the bride and the love of God for the church, parallels which are not just tolerated but inspired by the scriptures and tradition of the church.

The art critic Leo Steinberg has convincingly shown a whole artistic tradition during the Renaissance which seemed to be obsessed by the genitalia of Jesus.[9] Every picture displays the penis and testicles of the child and often has either the mother or some onlooker pointing to or even fingering these. During the crucifixion and at burial there is an emphasis on the genital area of the crucified, which shows that he was really human, not just a God in disguise. More striking and perhaps more disturbing to the iconoclasts and the puritans, says Greely commenting on this research, are those Renaissance artists who 'depict the risen Jesus as sexually aroused, that indeed he comes out of the tomb in these paintings with an erect penis, covered by bulging loincloth.'[10] This leads us to the topic of the next chapter which is the artistic channel in the Christian tradition.

Notes

1   Frederick Forsythe, *Emeka* (Ibaden, Spectrum Books, 1982). cf. Emeka Odumegwu-Ojukwu, *Because I am involved* (Ibaden, 1989).

2   John Cassian, *De Incarnatione* VI, 3; cf. St Augustine, *De Symbolo* 1; St Cyril of Jerusalem, Catechesis V,12.

3   Fyodor Dostoevsky, *The Brothers Karamazov*, vol. I (5) (Penguin Books, 1969), p. 298.

4   ibid., pp. 298-308.

5   Hans Georg Gadamer, *Truth and Method* (1989), p. 289.

6   Mark Patrick Hederman, *The Haunted Inkwell* (Dublin, Columba Press, 2001).

7   Andrew Greeley, *Religion as Poetry* (Transaction Publishers, 1995).

8   ibid., p. 43.

9   Leo Steinberg, *The Sexuality of Christ in Renaissance Art and in Modern Oblivion* (New York, Pantheon/October, 1983).

10 Andrew Greeley, *The Catholic Imagination* (University of California Press, 2000), p. 71.

CHAPTER TWO

Christianity and Art

ARTISTS HAVE HAD a pre-eminent place in Christianity since its foundation. Artists wrote the Gospels, artists created the specific form of Christian art in the icons, artists built and decorated the cathedrals of Christendom. Early Christianity had very little art. Coming from Judaism and being a proscribed religion in Rome it placed little emphasis on works of art. All that survives is sepulchral art – art made for cemeteries. In Rome the Christian dead were buried in underground chambers connected by narrow passages. This network of cubiculae became known as the catacombs. Rome today hosts 550 miles of these.

In 312 the emperor Constantine gave his official support to Christianity. He had seen a cross in the sky and been promised that under this sign he would conquer. Which he did. Eighteen years later he moved the capital of his empire to Byzantium, a small town on the sea of Marmora which he called Constantinople after himself. More recently, in 1930 Kemel Ataturk changed its name to Istanbul.

Byzantium was where Greek and Roman art met Asian influence and produced the essentially Christian Byzantine art, characterised most specifically by the icon. Icons are essentially a Christian art form. The word comes from the Greek word for an image, and it echoes the words used in the Bible to describe the creation of man and woman in the image of God. Those who are Christians, and who venerate the icons, believe that the Spirit guiding the creation of icons is the same that guided the creation of the world – The Holy Spirit, the Third Person of the Blessed Trinity. A beautiful ode dating from about 10 BC and attributed to King Solomon tells us:

> As the hand moves over the zither
> and the strings speak,
> so does the Spirit of the Lord
> speak in my limbs
> and I speak through his love.

Early Christian art was also painted as a fresco or built as a mosaic. The former were painted on masonry coated with layers of plaster (al fresco = while the plaster was still fresh or wet); the latter were composed of tiny cubes of coloured stone or glass pressed into the plaster.

Not all Christians venerated the icons. Not all religions permit such use of art as a depiction of God. Judaism, from which Christianity was born, is vehemently opposed to any representation of the Godhead which would be a work of human hands. As dutiful heir to the Jewish tradition, the early Church inherited the belief in a God who is, and must always be, beyond our imagining and our powers of description. This remains a constant bedrock of all Judeo-Christian teaching and is a natural attitude of a religion which was characterised by a tradition, over a thousand years old before ever Jesus Christ appeared, forbidding any images of God, even images formed in the mind, even the use of the name of God. Such prohibitions are enshrined in the decalogue: 'You shall not make yourself a graven image or any likeness whatever . . .'[1].

It is easy to understand, therefore, how the history of the icon is intimately bound up with the history of Christianity in the first centuries after Christ's death, as the community of Christians tried to work out the precise meaning of the tradition they had inherited: where it was the same as the Jewish tradition and where it differed.

One of the most important moments in this history of discovery of their authentic profile was the iconoclastic crisis. This has been compared with the later crisis in Christendom occasioned by what has become known as 'The Reformation' in the sixteenth century.

Iconoclasm means in Greek 'the smashing of images'. This movement of reform and purification in the Christian Church began in the first quarter of the eighth century, around 725. In this phase of the movement icons were destroyed as pagan images or idols, incompatible with Christian belief and a scandal to Jews and Moslems. In the second phase of the movement, almost a century later, icons were tolerated for pedagogical purposes, almost as a bible in pictures or comic strips, to teach the illiterate, but they were considered unsuitable for public worship and required to be removed from churches.

And, certainly, I find it very easy to understand the iconoclastic movement in the early church. When I see some of the hideous monstrosities that inhabit many Roman Catholic churches, when I hear of statues of the Child of Prague being buried in the garden to have a nice day for the wedding; pictures of Christ wearing a 'sacred heart' like a three dimensional valentine card pinned to his shirt; or the statues, pictures, plastic bottles with blue tops, of the Mother of God, which fall off the tables of overnight vendors in every shrine of the virgin the world over; bleeding statues, moving statues and even statues that drink nine spoonfuls of milk a day, one in Cheshire in England and one in Kuala Lumpur; embellished shrines in Knock, Medjugorje, Lourdes and in Chestakova in Poland, where the portrait of Our Lady, known as the Black Madonna, was supposedly painted by St Luke on boards taken from the table on which they ate the last supper! I sympathise with the Emperor Leo III, who undoubtedly initiated the iconoclastic movement in about 726. He may have had all kinds of political or economic reasons for doing so, but, to be fair to him, it seems to me that his basic reason was to institute a religious reform which would bring Christianity back to its roots, where worship in spirit and in truth would be the norm.[2] He looked around him and saw huge progress being made by the Moslem version of religion, which was emphatically and violently faithful to the principle of imagelessness. Not even animals could be depicted in their places of worship, not to speak of divine persons. Had there not been an earthquake in 726 which could only be an expression of Divine displeasure at the state of Christendom as he presided over it? Just as the earth had swallowed up Dathan for idolatrous practices, so the earth was swallowing up Christians who had strayed from the path of monotheistic purity.

Leo saw himself as prefigured in the Old Testament by Hezekiah, who destroyed the bronze serpent over the temple in Jerusalem eight hundred years after it had been put there as an object of worship – it being the one Moses had used to stem the plague of serpents in the desert. He, Leo, eight hundred years after Christianity was born would perform a similar symbolic act by destroying the bronze image of Christ which was above the entrance to his palace. Thus he would begin the work of saving Christianity from the idolatry which had crept in to despoil the original years of simplicity.

During the attempt to destroy these images, which had crept into Christianity by the eighth century, Leo III had a number of remarkable military successes over the, up to then, irresistible advance of Islam, which he took as confirmation from the Almighty of the direction he had initiated. So, Leo's son, in turn, the Emperor Constantine V, something of an amateur theologian, decided to copperfasten his father's endeavours by calling a Church Council which would endorse the principles of iconoclasm. There were 338 bishops at this council which met in Constantinople from 2 February to 8 August 754. Afterwards, it was suggested that the emperor put undue pressure on the bishops present, but whether he did or didn't, the council ratified the iconoclastic charter which was then promulgated by the Emperor.

Now, many later historians and believers hold that this was a high moment for Christianity and that if the results of this Council had been upheld we wouldn't have had to go through the later 'reformations' which proved so devastating to the unity of Christianity. However, history is written by the winners and the fact is that iconoclasm was defeated, the above Council declared heretical, and icons, images, statues, holy pictures, and representations of Christ, the Holy Family, the extended family of saints and angels were not just allowed back into our churches and dwelling-places but were declared to be an essential part of our Christian heritage.

This war was not won without a great deal of struggle, time, argument and even bloodshed. It took centre stage as the most important battle in Byzantium for nearly a century. Two Councils of the Church were devoted to it entirely until eventually in 787 the movement of iconoclasm was definitively defeated and icons were restored to their rightful place in the Christian scheme of things. So great a victory was hailed by the Church as a new feastday of Orthodoxy which to this day is celebrated in the Orthodox Church on the first Sunday of every season of Lent.

And most denominations of Christianity are involved in this declaration, including Roman Catholicism, because it was pronounced by the Seventh Ecumenical Council, held in Nicea from 24 September to 23 October and gained eventual recognition by the five great patriarchates of the time: Alexandria, Antioch, Constantinople, Jerusalem and Rome. It states:

> We retain, without introducing anything new . . . the representation of painted images . . . because of the belief in the true and non-illusory Incarnation of God the Word, for our benefit. For things which presuppose each other are mutually revelatory.
>
> Since this is the case, following the royal path and teaching divinely inspired by our Holy Fathers and the Tradition of the Catholic Church – for we know that it is inspired by the Holy Spirit who lives in it – we decide in all correctness and after a thorough examination, that, just as the holy and vivifying cross, similarly the holy and precious icons painted with colours . . . should be placed in the holy churches . . . on walls, on boards, in houses and on roads, whether these are icons of our Lord and Saviour, Jesus Christ, or our Spotless and Sovereign Lady, the holy Mother of God, or the holy angels and holy and venerable saints . . .

This Council had many repercussions, among which was a new understanding of ecumenicity. By declaring heretical the previous council summoned by the Emperor Leo III, it showed that validation of a council was not dependent upon either the authority of the emperor, or the presence of representatives of any or all of the major patriarchates of the Christian world, even if these signed the results unanimously. It was also necessary that the decrees promulgated should be accepted by the churches. In other words 'the effective ecumenicity of a council came to be mainly a process of assimilation by each church of the defined dogmatic orientations and of the canonical dispositions promulgated by the Council Fathers. Only when it becomes part of the liturgical life and ordinary catechetic teachings of each church does a Council acquire substantial ecumenicity.'[3]

Such was the context of this milestone in the evolution of Christianity, which had political as well as ecclesiastical repercussions that are still being felt today. More important for us is the content of the promulgation. It links the icons to the incarnation. If Jesus Christ actually became man and lived an historical life on earth then it must be possible to depict that life and represent his features in pictorial form. Just as the evangelists were able to write down an account of his life and his person in books which have become the definitive scriptures of Christianity, so, too, it must be possible for visual artists to describe Him in paint.[4] The VIIIth Ecumenical Council (869–870) goes so far as to say: 'The icon of Our Lord and Saviour Jesus Christ should be venerated with esteem equal to that afforded to the book of the holy gospels.'[5]

It was Constantine V, son of the Emperor Leo III who best expressed the difficulty of icon painting: 'We ask you how is it possible to depict our Lord Jesus Christ who is only one person of two natures, immaterial and material, through their union without confusion?' In other words, he was posing the dilemma for the defenders of icons that if they said the icon was depicting Christ as man only, they were guilty of Nestorianism, the great heresy which separated the human element from the divine; if they said the icon represented Christ as both God and man, they were guilty of the monophysite heresy which refused to separate the incomprehensible divinity from the humanity.

The art of the icon was the creative response to this dilemma. It is possible to depict this mystery, but no method of artistic representation which existed to date could do so. It was necessary to invent one appropriate to the challenge, which is what happened in Byzantium. Byzantium devised a new art form in the icon, but also through its architecture, which stands even today as what Goethe called 'frozen music' of eternity, capable of incarnating two completely different natures in one hybrid form. It is almost as if the art form devised was a visible defeat of two of the three laws of logical thought: both the principle of identity and the principle of non-contradiction: Everything is what it is and cannot, at the time it is what it is, be something else. And a thing 'A' cannot be both 'A' and not 'A' at the same time. Icons are both what they are and what they are not at the same time. This is not just a magical trick or an ancient form of *trompe-l'oeil* art, it is a unique and *sui generis* art form which incorporates the paradox upon which Christianity is founded, namely the mystery of the Incarnation, whereby a fragment of the created world becomes the embodiment of a world beyond.

Of course the artists must use the same materials and methods that other artists use. In fact, icons owe a great deal to the contemporary artistic methods used for making effigies of emperors and other funereal monuments both in ancient Egypt and in Rome.[6] However, this does not mean that the iconographers of Byzantium did not succeed in doing something entirely new with these same materials and using these contemporary models, just as Joyce in *Finnegans Wake* stretched language to another level of being and consciousness by his demanding use of it, even though he produced in the end a book which is printed in words by any average printing press. The icons of Byzantium forced artistic expression to perform a religious event which had never been as delicately encompassed in a work of art before that time. They fashioned out of wood and paint and lines and colours a way of encountering the face of Christ.

Many people, including William Butler Yeats, would claim that Byzantium was the place and the time when religious and artistic genius conspired to produce the highest form of art possible on this planet. In *A Vision*, Yeats wrote that Justinian's construction of the Cathedral of Hagia Sophia (CE 560) in Constantinople was one of history's closest approximations to absolute beauty as he understood it. 'Byzantium substituted for formal Roman magnificence, with its glorification of physical power, an architecture that suggests the Sacred City in the Apocalypse of St John. I think if I could be given a month of Antiquity and leave to spend it where I chose, I would spend it in Byzantium.' And he specifies that this art makes religious truths 'show as a lovely flexible presence like that of a perfect human body.'[7]

This was the time when these two creative sources of inspiration, art and religion, worked hand in hand to overcome a problem never before encountered in the history of humanity: the mystery of God appearing in human form. Language had to be contorted and adapted over four centuries of intensive understanding to find words which could express this incommunicable event; art made parallel strides to undertake such representation in its own idiom.

Icon painters work according to strict rules and canons laid down for such painting and have to be people of prayer and contemplation who are able to discipline themselves into a frame of mind and a state of soul that allows them to be in direct contact, in their own lives, with that same spirit which they are trying to release in the work of revelation they are undertaking.

It is for these reasons that icon painting was usually undertaken in monasteries by monks of both sexes, who

remained anonymous. Icons were not signed because the artist
was cooperating with the Holy Spirit.

So, what is it about the icons that is so special, so different.
First of all their subject matter. This can be divided into three
main categories, although others have extended this list to five
and more. They are scenes from the bible, both old and new
testaments, which have a didactic purpose, as one might see on
the great stained glass windows of so many Gothic cathedrals
also. They are portraits, although not in the same sense that we
have come to understand portrait painting since the sixteenth
century and up to our own times. And they are 'apparitional'.
This last description refers to those depicting all aspects of the
mystery of the Incarnation, which surpasses anything that can
be accounted for in the natural order and depicts the
intertwining of the divine and the human as such a history
unfolds in human terms. Icons depicting the Mother of God are
of this kind, as are depictions of the Transfiguration, the
Resurrection, the Baptism of the Lord, etc. Such icons, because
they break through the norms and boundaries of natural
existence, are often perceived to be sources of Divine
intervention and are accorded even greater veneration than
those in the first two categories.

The essence of the icon is the intuition that Yeats also
pinpointed – the image of God is actually to be found in the
human person. 'God created humankind in the image and
likeness of Himself' as the book of Genesis puts it. And Christ
is the perfect realisation of this truth. Karl Rahner expresses this
theologically in the phrase: 'All anthropology is deficient
Christology.'

And so, most icons are representations of human beings as
revelations of the image of God; of human faces as the veils on
which the imprint of divinity is most delicately sealed. And
finally, of the eyes of human beings, as the most translucent

and transparent windows to the soul, or that divine and infinite dimension of every human person: the eyes as doors of perception, windows to another world.

The icon is not a portrait in our sense. It is somewhere between this and a representation of the hidden beauty of each one of us, sometimes known only to those who fall in love with us, sometimes captured in an unselfconscious moment in a photograph when we say: 'That's me at my best'. Or, more often, other people say: 'That's really you', 'That's a great picture of you', 'That's you as you really are'.

> O sages standing in God's holy fire
> As in the gold mosaic of a wall,
> Come from the holy fire, perne in a gyre,
> And be the singing-masters of my soul.
> Consume my heart away; sick with desire
> And fastened to a dying animal
> It knows not what it is; and gather me
> Into the artifice of eternity.

The third verse of Yeats' famous poem 'Sailing to Byzantium' describes both the subject and the method of icon painting. There is an artifice, a trick, a method for conveying in paint and in picture the essential and the sacred features of the human face, of the human person, and once these have been released from the alienating features, the wrinkles and the twists, which suffering and evil inflict and thereby distort, they can become a radiant image of what they were originally intended to be.

This has been described theologically by Florensky, one of the great Russian theologians: 'Whatever is occasional or conditioned by outer circumstances, whatever does not belong to the true "face" is put aside by the energy of the image of God which, like a spring, has broken its way through the thickness of the material crust thus turning a face into the image. An image is a graphic reflection of the likeness of God on a human face.'⁹

So, how is this achieved? The first thing is to make us aware of how it is not achieved and to unveil the expectant prejudices of our own culture and upbringing. Most of us were brought up to expect a painting to look like the thing it was depicting. We liked to see on the canvas or in the picture an exact representation of what we see around us. The experience of the twentieth century has at least revealed to us the possibility that art is not necessarily like that. In fact, if we go now to an art exhibition anywhere in the world we are likely to be confronted by a series of pieces that look like nothing on earth: bits of twisted metal, blobs of scattered paint, geometrical and abstract shapes, brushes stuck upside down in paint buckets. This is contemporary art, we are told, don't be so fuddy-duddy, don't be looking for comfortable and comforting pictures of what is around you in your own life. You can get photographs if you want that kind of realism. Art is meant to shake you out of your smug, bourgeois, three-dimensional world and shock you into seeing another reality, and so on.

And in the face of all this fashionable talk, most of us prefer secretly to return to the older pictures in the gallery and to feast on the paintings we can recognise, the ones that show a horse or a dog, or people with umbrellas, or trees and flowers and people we can empathise with reading love-letters or working in fields.

And this preference is not 'natural'. It is, in fact, the result of a direction taken by the great masters of European art in and around the sixteenth century, especially when the extraordinary geometrical trick of perspective was invented by drawing lines in a deceptive way on a flat piece of paper or a square of canvas. Artists were able to fool us into thinking that we were looking

at an exact representation of the reality we saw around us. And
so fooled were we that we came to identify these paintings with
reality and with the only possible way to be an artist.

And it was, in fact, this wonderful world that these painters
were trying to capture perfectly in their works of art. It was
nature as science and common sense were able to understand
it, not the speculations about another world beyond or a
supernature or two natures mixed together in one.

Vasari, a painter who was Michelangelo's contemporary and
one of the first to write biographies of great painters of his
time, gives us a very revealing account of how Cimabue
discovered Giotto, who is sometimes identified as the person in
whom and through whom western European painting took this
'naturalistic' turn:

> [Giotto] while his sheep were grazing, was drawing one
> of them from life with a roughly pointed piece of stone
> upon a smooth surface of rock, although he had never
> had any master but Nature. . . . [A]ssisted by his native
> talent and taught by Cimabue, the boy not only equalled
> his master's style in a short time, but became such a good
> imitator of Nature that he entirely abandoned the rude
> Byzantine manner and revived the modern and good
> style of painting.[10]

We would not see Giotto as the epitome of the 'modern and
good style of painting', nor would we see the Byzantine style as
'rude', however it is not possible not to note the change of
direction which was taking place. The Renaissance was the
rebirth of Greek and Roman styles of art and even though the
themes and personalities were still borrowed from the Hebrew
and New Testament Bibles, the style was entirely natural and
human. This was the Classical style, embodying the ideal forms

of Plato and providing an aesthetic of perfect human and natural beauty. Harmony, balance of form and clarity of expression gave shape to the new humanism which turned away from the exclusively theological bias of medieval culture and concentrated on human achievements in the arts and science. It accompanied a revival of Classical learning, art and above all architecture. This entire movement, which started in Italy in the fourteenth century and spread from there to Northern Europe, flourished until the sixteenth century.

The incredible burgeoning of genius during this period seemed to provide the appropriate artists to carry the movement to unprecedented heights of originality and excellence. The Dominican Fra Angelico (1400–1455) remained in the contemplative tradition while adopting the new naturalistic style. Vasari tells us that he 'would never retouch or correct his pictures, leaving them always just as they had been painted. That, he used to say, was how God wanted them. It is also said that he would never take up his brushes without a prayer. Whenever he painted a crucifixion the tears would stream down his face'.[11]

Botticelli (1445–1510) retains in his huge number of paintings a symbolic reference system which is theological and religious but he has conquered the practical difficulties of depth perspective which remove from his rooms and spaces the awkwardness with regard to depth which we still find in Giotto. He like many of his contemporaries were obsessed with 'the investigation of difficult and impossible questions of perspective' to quote Vasari once again.

Leonardo Da Vinci (1452–1519) must be one of the most famous artists of all time. His *Last Supper* and *Mona Lisa* are two of the most discussed works ever painted. However, he did not consider himself to be a painter. 'He is entirely wrapped up in geometry and has no patience for painting' a visitor who met him in 1501 later reported. Leonardo was more of an inventor and a scientist than an artist in his own eyes. Sending his curriculum vitae to a potential employer in 1493 he lists nine of his accomplishments in engineering and warfare before he mentions that he can also 'give perfect satisfaction and to the equal of any other in architecture' and 'can carry out sculpture in marble, bronze or clay, and also I can do in painting whatever may be done.' In fact he did relatively few paintings. His interest was in science and his passion was for geometry and the perfection of the geometrical trick of perspective whereby paintings on a two dimensional surface could give the vivid and convincing impression of representing three-dimensional reality. He was also fascinated by the invention of machines for attacking and defending in times of war: 'Here the operation of bombardment might fall, I would contrive catapults, mangonels, trabocci and other machines of marvellous efficacy and not in common use'.

Michelangelo (1475–1564) is probably the most famous of them all. He was almost ninety when he died and the amount of work he carried out in every branch of artistic endeavour from his sonnets to St Peter's is quite phenomenal. Vasari waxes eloquent:

> The benign ruler of heaven graciously looked down to earth, saw the worthlessness of what was being done . . . and resolved to save us from our errors. So he decided to send into the world an artist who would be skilled in each and every craft . . . Moreover, he determined to give this artist the knowledge of the true moral philosophy and the gift of poetic expression, so that everyone might admire and follow him as their perfect exemplar in life, work and behaviour . . . and he would be acclaimed as divine. And therefore he chose to have Michelangelo

born a Florentine, so that one of her own citizens might
bring to absolute perfection the achievements for which
Florence was already justly renowned.

Raphael (1483–1520) was probably the artist who provided that
synthesis of order and science that gave the Western medieval
church a formula for what became a predictable and insulated
aesthetic. This was a Church rather than a religious aesthetic.
Raphael's Madonna became almost standardised: the
recognised and acceptable face, shape and arrangement of the
mother of God. Such endorsement of one particular art form
had a double effect. It meant that autonomous sources of
creative endeavour were effectively marginalised and
mainstream art within the church became imitative and
derived. With the passing of time and the development of
artistic reproductive technologies these original, and in
themselves, outstanding models became weaker and paler,
until they eventually became the mass-production of 'holy
pictures' which today clutter our stalls of religious
pornography and the shrines of our religious imagination.

Caravaggio (1573–1610) takes his name from the place near
Bergamo where he was born. His real name was Michelangelo
Merisi. He was probably the artist most responsible for moving
the Renaissance in the direction of full naturalistic realism and
humanism. Although his paintings are commissioned by
members of the Church hierarchy and ostensibly portray
figures familiar to us from the Bible, they are situated squarely
within an unrelenting and unrelieved human situation and
setting. The artist himself had a violent temperament and
throughout his life was involved in physical brawls, had
constant tensions with the authorities, and spent time in prison.
His art was as violent and as disrespectful of authority as
himself. His commissions being mostly for religious works he

created a highly original religious style. His works have a startlingly direct and dramatic appeal to the spectator, with a very palpable sense of the complex and pitiable plight of human beings. His first version of St Matthew on the altarpiece in oil on canvas for the Contarelli Chapel paintings was rejected by the clergy as improper: Matthew was a burly peasant whose dirty feet stuck out of the painting almost as an insult to the spectator. In *The Calling of St Matthew*, the would-be saint with his grubby and lascivious gambling partners show various complex psychological reactions to the appearance of Christ in their midst. All these paintings present a vivid narrative realism which would have been shocking to an audience accustomed to Raphael's delicate idealisations. Plebeian characters, grim surroundings, stark lighting techniques and overcast claustrophobic settings and spaces, made these works seem irreligious to his contemporaries. The Carmelite nuns rejected the Death of the Virgin which had been commissioned for them when they were presented with what amounted to a bloated corpse.

Whatever about the merits or the results of this new kind of Church art, it sprang from a very different kind of theology. A new age was here, one which was interested in emotional expression, in psychological reality, in how real people looked and felt and conducted their lives. The technique of oil painting allowed Christian art to take on the most dramatic and picturesque expressions and settings. Raphael, Leonardo da Vinci and Michelangelo expressed a beauty and a realism that were stunningly impressive, but, at the same time, were part of that renaissance which eventually led to a world around us sufficient in and to itself, without any windows opening to a divine reality of equal but entirely different proportions, perspectives and perceptibility. Caravaggio carried this realism to its most startling and exquisite perfection.

In the art of the Renaissance it is the spectator who is the centre of the composition. The world is on display for your benefit, from your perspective as consumer. Such a development can only be understood in terms of the parallel history of the papacy which accompanied the lives and works of the artistic geniuses that adorned nearly two centuries of Roman history.

There were no less than twelve popes during Michelangelo's lifetime. Some of these were his greatest sponsors, promoters and employers, others were determined to remove, or at least cover over, what they saw as his blasphemous and obscene desecration of their most sacred shrines. In fact, the panoramic ceiling of nudity which covered the Sistine Chapel has never been seen as it was originally intended and executed; even the most recent restoration failed to remove some of the lingerie superimposed by papal decree to cover the pudenda and offensive protuberances of (mostly) damned humanity, which might effect too much delight in the eyes of the beholder.

The two popes who were probably the most influential in their support of the fruitful crossfertilisation between the Church and the great artists of the Italian Renaissance were Julius II (Pope from November 1503 to February 1513) and Leo X (March 1513– December 1521). Julius issued from one of the most corrupt periods in the history of the papacy, being the enemy of Alexander VI, probably the most notorious pope of all time, and being himself elected after his predecessor, Pius III, resigned only twenty-six days after his elevation, with the help of lavish promises and bribes at a conclave lasting only a single day. He was a forceful, ruthless and violent ruler who set out to extend the papal state. He lead a military campaign with himself in full armour at its head which returned Perugia and Bologna to his jurisdiction. Historians allow him military prowess but award him few marks for his priesthood. He was self-willed, easily angered and sensual. As Cardinal he had fathered three children and was called '*Il terribile*'. However, on his death he was hailed by Italians as the one who freed their country from foreign domination.

As patron of the arts he sponsored Michelangelo and Raphael among others. He laid the foundation stone for the new St Peter's and arranged for the cost to be defrayed by selling indulgences. His successor, Leo X, was a polished renaissance prince who was also a masterly politician. He was recklessly extravagant, sold ecclesiastical offices and even cardinal's hats to pay for his projects. To pay for the huge expense of St Peter's he renewed the indulgences authorised by Julius and arranged for these to be promoted by preachers throughout Christendom. It was in January 1517 that the notorious John Tetzel began his preaching outreach to Germany. Is it any wonder that the iconoclasm of Martin Luther (1483–1546) began also to have effect at these times.

The Eastern Tradition, especially as this comes down to us in the specific art of the icons, did not travel that road of realism, naturalism and geometrically achieved perspective. Nor was this for reasons of ignorance, chauvinism, stuffy conservatism or lack of inventive ability. It was because they believed that the art form which they had inherited was the one most appropriate to the task of expressing the most important realities in their lives. These realities did not concern simply the everyday world in which we live, even if this could become the theatre for more elevated and mystical emotions, but embodied an existence which was wider, larger, taller and deeper than the three-dimensional one so admirably captured on the Renaissance canvasses.

In the art of the Renaissance it is the spectator who is centre of the composition. Everything is depicted from your point of view as if you happened to be the privileged witness stumbling in on the scene before you. As spectator you slot into the place marked out for you in front of the painting. The work of art begins to work its magic in the precise place and at the right distance in front of you. It unfolds a scene in front of you as if you were there, a contemporary witness. Caravaggio, for instance, dressed his figures in clothes of his own time and fashion.

In the icon, the figure of Christ, the Virgin or the Saint or whatever is being represented, is the centre. The viewer is faced with a reversed perspective and it is the icon that is beholding you, not the other way round. This is why most figures are in a frontal position, with eyes gazing outwards like laser beams. Instead of being the source or starting-point of the picture as in perspectival painting, the beholder is the culminating or vanishing point of the icon.

There is little or no psychology or drama going on within the icon itself that I can pry upon like a voyeur from the outside; most of the energy is being generated between the spectator and the figures in the icon itself. The place in whose forehead the gaze of the icon opens is you yourself. You are arrested in the Garden of your own particular Gethsemane.

In the icon we do not see God as an object to be contemplated but as a subject contemplating us as viewers. Thus, the icon does not try to represent God as He is in Himself, but as He appears to us.

Technically speaking, there is no shadow, therefore, in the world of the icon. We do not find the subtle play of light and darkness we have become so familiar with and enchanted by in European painting. The layer of goldleaf which is the basis for many icons is the most fundamental symbol of the presence of God as light. Gold is not really a colour, strictly speaking, it is a surface which eliminates all illusion of an intermediary space between it and the forms embedded in it: it is pure context. It absorbs into itself other light, even that emanating from other colours.

By all such methods icons are means of communication. They radiate an energy of light. They are not meant to create pious sentiments and/or psychological moods in the viewer, they are meant to be the most immediate (without media) communication: windows into another world.

The icon has no frame. It is not self-contained. It is open to the infinite on all sides. It is merely a focal point, a prism, concentrating energy and relaying vision to a place beyond itself. The fact that it is a flat material surface is dissolved by the artistry accomplished on and through that surface. The phosphorescence and the stillness act as a tranquilliser that should link us to the still point of the turning world.

The Renaissance introduces another world. It represents the actual world in which we live. Both kinds of art can be 'religious' and each method of working can be effective as a vehicle for the Spirit. The more conceptual and abstract art of the icons emphasises the otherworldly and divine aspect of Christianity, whereas the down to earth more human treatment of the Renaissance artists emphasises the flesh and blood humanity of both Christ and his followers. In both cases it is the artist who infuses the style with its theological and religious intensity and validity.

Pope John-Paul II in his 'Letter to Artists' has made it clear that art can be and has been a vehicle for theology, not just an illustration of, or a companion to, theology. Just as in the Eastern Orthodox Church the icons of Andrei Roublev (1360–1430), especially his depiction of The Trinity, are regarded as theological works, so too have artists of all ages been inspired by the Holy Spirit to manifest the divinity.

However, the even more important point is that we as inheritors of the Renaissance and as educated citizens of

Europe during the last two centuries have inherited a prejudice and almost genetically received an inborn bias in favour of the second kind of art which was naturalistically real. During the twentieth century two sources of education helped to unveil this as a prejudice and cause us to readjust our way of seeing things. The first of these was the invention of the photograph and the second was the new art which was being foisted upon us by the geniuses of our own times.

The long and dedicated working history which allowed artists to move from where Giotto started to where Caravaggio produced a perfection of perspectival geometry and natural realism that seemed inspired, could now be reproduced even more perfectly by a machine. Artists knew then that the mystery of reality lay elsewhere, that the semblance of reality was a well disguised trick.

The cinema, which was a form of art invented by the twentieth century, was immediate prey to this prejudice. The cinema became one long visual attempt to reproduce the naturalistic art of realism over an extended showing. Two kinds of 'religious' cinema emerged: one could be called sensational, the other sentimental. Both used the themes, the personalities, the conventions and the techniques of high Renaissance art. The sensational variety harnessed all the gimics and virtuosity of cinematic technology to represent the miraculous and the interventionist efforts of an external divinity. The sentimental versions present the lives of the saints and of Christ on earth as a Palestinian version of the lives everyone leads: Christ in Coronation Street, Mary as the girl next door.

The kind of cinematography which could adapt itself to the art form of the icon is illustrated in the work of the French director Robert Bresson (1907–1999). In a small book called *Notes on Cinematography*[12] written in 1975 he makes a basic distinction between his work, which he calls 'cinematography', and 'cinema' as most had experienced this art form up to that date. Cinema is no more than photographed theatre. Cinema uses the camera to reproduce; cinematography uses it to create. In the world of theatre everything is necessarily artificial. You don't expect to find real trees growing on the stage. Scenery is an artificial construction. Acting, in the idiom of theatre, has to participate in such artificiality. It is a calculated method. Bresson hopes that cinematography can introduce us to something original, not merely photographed theatre but a language of the screen. Bresson gave up using professional actors unable to shake off 'the terrible habit of theatre'. He uses instead what he calls 'models' who are completely innocent of all methods, techniques or poses of 'professional' acting. With regard to such models: 'the thing that matters is not what they show me but what they hide from me, and, above all, what they do not suspect is in them.'

Cinema should be the subtlest and most versatile of all the arts at presenting the essence of a human being. Beyond acting and seeming there is a reality which, now and then, we catch a glimpse of and which the camera should be ever on the alert to record. This 'being' of the person is the real quarry of the cinematographer and it is hidden by a conscious project on the part of either actors or scriptwriters. It is there in all of us, but rarely seen, except when sometimes revealed by an involuntary gesture, a ripple from the unconscious, which the camera can capture if ready and not distracted. The director prepares the scene for this revelation and then awaits the epiphany. All other considerations are unworthy of this art-form now at our disposal. And yet, in Bresson's view, we galvanise the whole industry to record the banalities which are our own pathetically constructed dramas. From the very first chapter of the Bible we have been told that 'the image of God' is to be found in the men and women he made in his own image and likeness. Until this century we had only succeeded in producing some cumbersome art forms to capture this mystery. Now we at last have an art form capable of tracking something of this mercurial essence, whether in a glance or a gesture, or a movement of the face. Such possibility made this particular director vow 'not to shoot a film in order to illustrate a thesis, or to display men and women confined to their external aspect, but to discover what they are made of, to attain that "heart of the heart" which does not let itself be caught either by poetry, or by philosophy or by drama' (p. 20). The image in a Bresson film must assume the technical humility of an icon which allows something other than the depiction to shine through. His aim is to slow down our frantic ransacking of the image for its narrative content and allow us to gaze at the reality itself: 'Against the tactics of speed, of noise, set the tactics of slowness, of silence' (p. 28). Speaking of the fundamental attitude of the cinematographer, he quotes the admonition 'Be attentive' from the Greek Orthodox liturgy, 'one must not seek, one must wait'; because the purpose of such films is to 'make visible what, without you, might never have been seen' (p. 39). Such an attitude must also apply to those who are in the film. Professionals tend to regard the eye of the camera as equivalent to the eye of the public and this gives their performance a realistic perspective which was the hallmark of the Renaissance. The beholder becomes the centre of attention and everything must be done to seduce that eye. Bresson seeks to focus attention on the mystery of the film itself. 'Build your film on white, on silence and on stillness' (p. 71); 'it all winds up on a rectangle of white fabric hung on a wall' which means that the film is 'a surface to cover' (p. 3). To his 'models' he gives the following instructions: 'It is to you, not to the public that they give those things which it, perhaps, would not see (which you glimpse only). A secret and a sacred trust' (p. 48). 'Your film's beauty,' he continues, 'will not be in the images (postcardism) but in the ineffable which they will emanate' (p. 61). Explaining this essential humility of the image Bresson tells a story he read in a newspaper:

> In London a gang broke open the safe in a jeweller's shop and laid hands on pearl necklaces, rings, gold, precious stones. They also found the key of the nearby jeweller's safe, which they cleaned out, and this safe contained the key of a third jeweller's safe. (p. 70)

The cinematographer has to stand by to rob each image, to clean it out of all its glittering superficiality, until it gives up its key which will open up the mystery of the next image. In this way he will keep the attention of the spectator fixed upon the essence of the reality which the film tries to transmit but which is inevitably elsewhere. Therefore the images used must be 'flat' and almost insignificant in themselves, like words in a dictionary, 'having no power and value except through their position and relation' (p. 5). The film is not a concatenation of independent images making up a narrative sequence, 'each image must be transformed by contact with other images as is a colour by contact with other colours' (p. 5). 'Your images will release their phosphorous only in the aggregate' (p. 44) so you have to see the film as 'a combination of lines and of volumes in movement apart from what it represents and signifies' (p. 44).

In an interview about his film *Un condamné à mort s'est échappé* (The Escape of a Prisoner Condemned to Death), whose subtitle was 'The wind blows where it will', Bresson said:

> I would like to show this miracle: an invisible hand over the prison, directing what happens and causing such a

thing to succeed for one and not for another . . . The film
is a mystery . . . The Spirit breathes where it will.[13]

The way he 'shows' this is not by explaining anything or
turning the story into a sensational thriller, it is, as Eric Rohmer
names it, by 'the miracle of objects'. Everything in the film
could be explained naturally. The prisoner seems to escape by
his own efforts, so much so that, at one point, Bresson was
tempted to call it 'God helps those who help themselves'.
However, there is another presence felt throughout the film
which never appears but which emanates from the objects, the
details, the persons and especially the images which unfold on
the screen. The escape of the prisoner is, in fact, a parable
about the escape of each image from its own circumscribed
death-cell into another kind of movement and life. The method
of such cinematography is 'to translate the invisible wind by
the water it sculpts in passing' (p. 36). Such cinematography
makes certain demands upon the audience:

> A highly compressed film will not yield its best at the first
> go. People see in it at first what seems like something
> they have seen before. (p. 65)

Bresson suggest that there should be places where in 'one quite
small, very well equipped cinema, only one or two films would
be shown each year' (p. 65).

Notes

1   Exodus: 20: 1–17: 'You shall not make yourself a carved image or any
    likeness of anything in heaven or on earth beneath or in the waters
    under the earth; you shall not bow down to them or serve them. For
    I, the Lord your God, am a jealous God . . .'

2 I am supported in these views of Iconoclasm by Christophe Schoenborn in *L'Icône du Christ, Fondements Théologiques* (Paris, 1986), from whom I borrow some of these thoughts.

3 Vittorio Peri, 'The Church of Rome and the Ecclesiastical Problems Raised by Iconoclasm', *Icons, Windows on Eternity, Theology and Spirituality in Colour*, compiled by Gennadios Limouris (Geneva, WCC Publications, 1990), p. 28–29.

4 cf. Colossians 1:15: 'He is the image of the invisible God' (where the Greek word used is 'icon') and Hebrews 1:3: 'He reflects the glory of God and bears the very stamp of his nature'.

5 Denzinger 653, p. 218. Can. 3. 'Sacram imaginem Domini nostri Jesu Christi et omnium Liberatoris et Salvatoris, aequo honore cum libro sanctorum Evangeliorum adorari decernimus.'

6 cf. Andre Grabar, *Christian Iconography, A Study of its Origins*, which were the A.W. Mellon Lectures in the Fine Arts at the National Gallery of Art in Washington in 1961 (Bollingen Series, Princeton University Press, 1968).

7 W.B. Yeats, *A Vision* (1937), p. 279.

9 P. Florensky, quoted in *Icons, Windows on Eternity*, op. cit., p. 155.

10 Giorgio Vasari, *The Lives of the Painters, Sculptors, and Architects* (New York, E.P. Dutton, 1927), I, p. 66.

11 Ibid., I, p. 206.

12 Robert Bresson, *Notes on Cinematography* (New York, Urizen Books, 1977).

13 *The Films of Robert Bresson* (London, Studio Vista, 1969) p. 68.

Chapter Three

Art as Education

ART, GENERALLY SPEAKING, is about the way we experience life through our five senses. Music for the ears, sculpture and painting for the eyes, and then all the literary arts for a population in contemporary Ireland, 70 per cent of whom, we are told, have had some kind of third-level education.

But let us go back to what we were and what we still are at other levels. For illiterate cultures the sense of smell was paramount and required the development of a whole art of aromatology. There was a huge contribution from the sense of smell to all social interaction. Sexual attraction has always been strongly associated with scent. The word orchid in Greek means testicle. So many so called deodorants for men are processed testicular juices from jaguars, cheetahs, macho-males from the jungle. Brand names such as 'lynx' and 'brute' leave little to the imagination.

However, when we approach the counter for female aromatherapy we are left quite speechless at the complexity of the olfactory code. The fragrance for an average perfume has over three hundred ingredients

Wherever we are on this planet, even while you are sitting or standing as you read this page in some insulated room, you are surrounded by at least half a million smells. And each of us is equipped with that unobtrusive and often cheekily attractive piece of equipment commonly referred to as the nose, which is really no more than a tube or a colander with about five million sniffer cells on either side. When describing a particular scent, however, we are trying to create an image in a smell space. I might say that yours has a peachy apricot flavour, whereas the more psychological among us might speak of its smoulderingly aggressive pungency. But the Yehudi Menuins of the perfume world will treat us to a whole scale of values in terms of musical notation in which the rose is your middle C and the top notes are the first impressions you get, lasting for no more than a few minutes, the middle notes are those that waft around you for about half an hour, and the bass notes are the ones that remain throughout the day. The essential facts are these: we are so constitutionally self-centred in the area of smell that we hardly notice, in fact we mostly enjoy, whatever odours issue from ourselves. We happily survive in rooms permeated with our own unrestricted farting, whereas we run with ostentatious fastidiousness from emporia where others have too loudly exercised the same privilege. We inhale the musky scent from the bodies of those we love; from others, especially those of a different ethnicity to ourselves, we detect a fetid stink.

If we move into the arena of taste, the art of cooking and of wine-tasting, for instance, you might be preparing your Taglioni Verde, *al dente*, with aubergines, tomato and garlic sauce, or serving your Australian red with deep-purple colour, warm fruity nose, ripe pepper and smooth tannins on the palate, its creamy depth, faultless balance and persistent length, for a monomaniacal meat-and-potatoes man or a plonk guzzler, and you are wasting your time. Note that the words used in the first half of the last sentence to evoke the beauty of food and wine are vocabulary borrowed from another medium, another sense language, to describe the less articulate region of taste.

Or if we move to the sense of touch, we enter a world of primary and instinctual communication. People who have the common touch, who can reach you with a handshake. People who find any touching very threatening. We all know the difference between touching something slimy, sticky, furry, alive, dead, putrid; walking barefoot through summer grass, sand, fresh cowdung. Pressing the flesh is compulsory for politicians and you cannot test the paintwork of my BMW with your gloves on. You've got to play it with the flesh at the top end of your fingers. That's what gives the personality and individuality to your sound if you are a musician, what makes the lute a more tactile instrument than the guitar. Larry Adler playing Gershwin's *Rhapsody in Blue* gives the saxophone a sensual connotation. A kiss on the hand may be quite continental but diamonds are a girl's best friend, because 'square cut or pear shape, these rocks don't lose their shape'.

Art is trying to elevate our taste. Which means that art is trying to change the 'natural' way we do things, see things. Art is essentially artificial. It is a set-up, a frame-up. It is a booby trap, a confidence-trick. It is a piece of stone pretending to be a human body. It is a piece of square cloth pretending to be an open field. It is a lighted box pretending to house a planet. It is a magic lantern flickering fantasies on a screen. Somehow it has to capture us and when we are caught it has to lead us into another world.

'Being natural is a pose' Oscar Wilde once said, 'and the most irritating pose I know.' Natural in Ireland, according to one local expert, 'is a crowd of the lads and they roaring laughing at somebody speaking French'. It is inevitably connected with being ignorant. The natural way of seeing the universe is quite different from the way things actually are. In fact, the greatest enemy of art is the 'common sense' view of the ordinary person. Most people imagine that great art, art down the centuries, the kind of art that you find in Rome, in Florence, in Paris, in the Tate Gallery and in the National Gallery of Ireland, represents reality as it really is. And then a crowd of anarchists and philistines who couldn't draw a revolver or paint a barn door took over the art schools and salons of Europe and began to force what they called 'modern' art down our throats. And now, instead of going back to what was right and what we know and what was recognisable as art, we've been pushed forward again into 'post-modern' art. The truth is that the kind of art most of us like, that we recognise and cherish, is a distortion. Far from showing us reality as it actually is, this kind of art flatters us by showing us reality as we 'naturally' imagine it to be, as we think it should be: the sentimental setting of a chocolate box world.

There are several kinds of art and there are several ways that art can function. There is an art of propaganda, an art of protest, an art of popular entertainment, an art which appeals, an art which provokes, an art which prophesies, an art which penetrates. So, in other words, there is an art which establishes us and confirms us in our own smug common-sense view of the world around us, and there is an art which shakes us up and shows us that the way we see things is not really the way things are.

Naturally, we are idealistic, we are sentimental. We love to sit and watch a good old-fashioned movie, where everybody is patriotic, every soldier is courageous, every priest is celibate, every bride is a virgin, every marriage is forever, every dog is everlasting, every hero is noble, upright, pure, and looks you straight in the eye. All that Enid Blyton, Beatrix (or maybe these days Harry) Potter, Biggles, Boy's Own, and Hollywood brought us up on. 'Blue skies, smiling at me, nothing but blue skies do I see'. We want the world to be like Disneyland, no matter how obviously and how consistently it is revealed to us as the opposite. And even though our 'post-modern' culture, linked to an all-pervasive, importunate, brash, unavoidable and incontrovertible communications technology, shows us all our heroes and every idol in the grim light of their human frailty we still want the fairytale, the Mills and Boon love story, the transatlantic rosemantic.

Art is trying to show us something different, something other. And yet it is true to say that its only real purpose is to show us what really is. It is not invention it is revelation, a vision of what actually is there before our eyes if we could see it. But, the truth is that we are blinded. Our vision is myopic, impeded, reduced. What we see is what we want to see. And so, even our 'art' is reduced to our own size. We like it to be comfortable. We also like our religious art to be confirming and supportive: Chocolate Box Christianity. Our set might include Rembrandt's *Prodigal's Son*, Millais' *The Angelus*, Leonardo's *Last Supper*, Botticelli's *Virgins*, a cluster of Raphael's and a magnum of Murillo's. Something akin to Irish-American travelogues about Ireland: *The Lakes of Killarney*, *The Turf-Cutter's Donkey*, *Galway Bay*, *The Blarney Stone*, *The Rose of Tralee*, and *The Quiet Man*.

Or else we look on art as an investment. We are obviously impressed that Van Gogh, who couldn't sell a painting during his lifetime except one to his brother, Theo, and who everyone dismissed as a nutcase, began selling for over £6,000,000 a throw, or rather an iris or a wilting sunflower, a hundred years after he painted them. If we could only separate the champions from the charlatans and work out which contemporary art-work might be sold in Christie's or Sotheby's in a hundred years time for six million ecus, we might even buy one ourselves.

When I walk down a street I don't see everything, I can't see everything. There are far too many things to see. I see what I am looking for. If I am hungry I see restaurants, I see food. If I

need petrol I see signs for petrol stations. If I want to park I see
empty spaces, or, rather, nowadays, the complete absence of
empty spaces, and so I look for 'P' signs. The eye is a curved
surface with 150 million photoreceptors embedded in the
retina. These are sensitive to light, which comes in packages of
photons: one photon of light enters each receptor. If there is no
light I see nothing. When I see a green leaf, for instance, what
really happens is that a 'white' light, normally from the sun,
falls on the tree, and also falls on my eye. Part of the light is
absorbed by the tree and part of it is refracted towards my eyes.
This stimulates in me the appropriate nerve, which transforms
the assault on my retina into the appropriate nervous energy
which travels along the optic nerve to the primary visual cortex
at the back of the brain. In other words the retina of the eye is
like a kind of skin which is, in fact, an outgrowth of the brain
and it is not the eye that sees it is the brain. The brain paints the
picture. What we call 'green' is really a combination of two
things: there is the green of the grass or the leaves outside our
mind and there is the green inside our minds which is an
electro-magnetic sensation interpreted by our minds. And this
interpretation is enshrouded in our own desires, our habits of
perception, and our usual expectations. We only have to look at
the thing under our foot for a second to know that it is only a
leaf and pass on. The mind immediately jumps to this
conclusion. If we are living in Africa, for instance, we might
wait another few seconds to make sure that it wasn't a snake.
Those who are my age will remember John Mills walking
through the desert in the film *Ice Cold in Alex* (which is now part
of an ad for beer). The desert was a minefield, left that way
deliberately by the enemy. Suddenly the hero stops and the
audience gasps as he says: 'There is something under my foot.'
And about half an hour later after much scraping of sand and
whispering and feeling around we all discover that it is an

empty can. But it could so easily have been something else, something more dangerous. The mind has to work it out.

It is the mind not the eye that sees. It is the brain that filters what we hear. It is the head that calculates what we feel. The medieval king in France who banished his court jester because he was too cheeky, telling him that if he ever again put his foot on French soil he would be executed, proved this point. The jester filled up a cart with German soil and standing on this drove back to the king's palace. 'I am here,' he mocked, 'but I am not standing on French soil'. The king decided to play a trick on him. He pretended to have his head chopped off but at the last minute he told the executioner to let a drop of water fall on his neck. The executioner did what he was told and when the king ran down to have a good laugh at the jester, he found that the jester was dead. The mind had supplied for what the experience had lacked. His mind had executed him.

'I hate green', you say, and this means that your mind is focusing not just on the present sensation but on memories and past experiences which have further coloured this colour with your own emotional involvement. Which means that there is no such thing as a 'standard' green. We only have to remember that some people are colour blind. This, at one end of the spectrum, where some cannot see colours at all. At the other end of the spectrum there are apparently 12 per cent of people who carry the gene for a kind of vision that is unusual, and which may be transmitted to their children. This makes their colour vision tetrachromatic rather than trichromatic. They have four rather than three kinds of cone in their retina which gives them the possibility of very subtle awareness of different mixtures of light. This allows them to reliably discern shades of green that you and I can hardly distinguish. They don't just sing about the forty shades of green in the landscape of Erin, they can actually see them and identify them: 'What was she wearing?' 'A green frock.' 'Emerald, verd-antique, malachite, beryl, bottle-green, aquamarine, olive, or verdigris?' The possibility is that Van Gogh was given such a gene by his mother. He shows us a world of greens that we are only now beginning to see because of him.

If we look at the last series of images which Cézanne painted of Mont Sainte-Victoire we find that our eyes are required to glide over a narrow foreground zone of green, over a wide flat plain of middle ground before reaching the mountain. 'The multicoloured weave of patches of colour in the middle ground, created by means of a vigorous interplay of broad brushstrokes, thin hatchings, and carefully placed, small, flat planes, links foreground, middleground and background by repeating the hues of the meadows and olive trees and the crystalline blues of the mountain. In this culmination of Cézanne's painting technique the motif often all but disappears in an intricate mass of colour gradations and paint layers.'[1]

Cézanne was trying to show us the difference between seeing and recognising. He was trying to slow down the process so that we could become aware of the colour impressions or sensations that are the way we see before the mind closes in and completes the picture. Cézanne shows us what he himself experienced and believed, that the eye does not see 'objects' or identifiable 'things'; what first appears is a multicoloured tapestry of 'tâches colorées' a patchwork quilt of colour, a batik of intermingling hues.

Cézanne teaches us how to see. Rather, as Lacan says, he makes us see what prevents us from seeing. What the object is masking, dissimulating by its massive, fascinating presence, is not some other positivity but its own place, the void, the lack that it is filling in by its presence – its fascinating presence is here just to mask the emptiness of the place it occupies (a kind of illusion). Cézanne's paintings are also metaphors for feelings.

Lacan compares this also to a potter who creates the vase with
his hand around this emptiness, starting with a hole.

Cézanne distinguished between seen and recognised reality
and limited himself to recording the actual process of vision; that
is, he tried to expunge from his mind all knowledge about the
things that he saw and to depict only the colour impressions – or
'sensations', as he called them – that those things made on his
eye. In so doing, Cézanne took a step into new perceptual realms.

> Treat nature by means of the cylinder, the sphere, and
> the cone, everything brought into proper perspective so
> that each side of an object or a plane is directed toward a
> central point. Lines parallel to the horizon give breadth .
> . . a section of nature . . . lines perpendicular to the
> horizon give depth. But nature for us is more depth than
> surface, whence the need to introduce into our light
> vibrations, represented by the reds and yellows, a
> sufficient amount of blueness to give the feel of air.[2]

> ....

> There mustn't be a single slack link, a single gap through
> which the emotion, the light, the truth can escape. I
> advance all of my canvas at one time, if you see what I
> mean. And in the same movement, with the same
> conviction, I approach all the scattered pieces . . .
> Everything we look at disperses and vanishes, doesn't it?
> Nature is always the same, and yet its appearance is
> always changing. It is our business as artists to convey the
> thrill of nature's permanence along with the elements
> and the appearance of all its changes. Painting must give
> us the flavour of nature's eternity. Everything, you
> understand. So I join together nature's straying hands . . .
> From all sides, here, there, and everywhere, I select
> colours, tones, and shades; I set them down, I bring them

together . . . They make lines. They become objects – rocks, trees – without my thinking about them. They take on volume, value. If, as I perceive them, these volumes and values correspond on my canvas to the planes and patches of colour that lie before me, that appear to my eyes, well then, my canvas 'joins hands'. It holds firm. It aims neither too high nor too low. It's true, dense, full . . . But if there is the slightest distraction, the slightest hitch, above all if I interpret too much one day, if I'm carried away today by a theory which contradicts yesterday's, if I think while I'm painting, if I meddle, then whoosh!, everything goes to pieces.[3]

A contemporary artist, Bridget Reilly, paints abstract canvases of vertical stripes or interlocking diamonds. Her aim is to convey to us pure sensation. What you see in a split second out of the corner of your eye before you focus attention and label the experience. She and other artists claim that we are essentially killers of reality, that the mind destroys, that we look around us as murderers looking for booty or prey, whatever we want to see we frame-freeze and gobble into our filing cabinets. We see what we already know. What we call 'seeing' is, in fact, reconstruction not just from fragmentary evidence glimpsed quickly as we survey the scene looking for clues, but from a whole wardrobe of accumulated past experiences which we immediately project onto the unsuspecting identity parade lined up in front of us. Experience is killed dead by recognition. The reality outside us is always transformed by what we are supplementing from the inside. We label everything and everyone. We are utility seekers, supermarket shoppers, who flatten sensation into a treasure hunt. We are on the alert for whatever is familiar, we lay traps for sensation so that all we catch is the prey we want. Our nets are designed to let everything else go free. We only want the big fish, the news that hits the headlines, the celebrity page, the movers and the shakers. We are carpetbaggers accumulating souvenirs, ratpackers collecting freebies, tourists amassing slides of life. Every time *Crimeline* displays the portrait of a potentially dangerous and wanted person at large, they get telephone calls from every part of the country from people who have seen this person. We see what we want to see, what we expect to see.

There are skills of our contemporary culture, known as speed-reading, sight-seeing, surfing the internet, and channel-hopping on television, all of which mean that you travel at speed until something captures your attention, catches your eye, punctures your eyeball, and then you stop and take a look. And what stops you in your tracks is what you yourself are already looking for, what you are anxious to see. At the social level it translates itself into celebrity spotting or fame scanning by society X-rays. You go to a party and engage, but only until you see someone more important on the horizon, then you disengage and you re-engage, all the time keeping a detached retina for the even more important personage who might appear. This is sight-seeing as we do it 'naturally'. We go to where the four stars are posted in the brochure, where we're likely to get the best value. Our natural gaze is predatory, calculating, selective, and selfish.

We must all recognise this. As we approach the breakfast table we are looking for eats. We don't care how beautiful the orange is – we don't see it like Cézanne. We shake the empty packet of flakes and throw it away, never pausing to see or to read what is on it. On the other hand, once we are seated and busily shovelling the chemicals into the hole in our head another factor takes over. The eye wanders and peripheral vision creeps forward. We begin to read in spite of ourselves the ads for holidays in the sun on the empty packet. This is the basic principle of advertising. Even if I don't notice it, it notices me. On the subway the pictures flashing by or the ones splattered on the walls sink in somewhere. These images resurface when I least expect them, in dreams or whenever I leave them space. So, there are two channels to our sensuality. There is what I see and what sees me. There is what I take in and what takes me in. Training the eye to see more than the immediate surface reality is a matter of education. Having passed down a street looking for something to eat and seeing only restaurants and food that was too expensive we arrive at the other end and our car is stopped. A policeman asks us to tell him what we saw. A murder was committed on that street as we were passing by. He is asking us to jog our memory, to retrace our steps. It is amazing how much we did see without really noticing it. We amaze ourselves with the variety and detail of our recall when we are forced to ransack our memory banks. Such an exercise shows us how little we use the senses at our disposal – we reduce these to tin-openers and strip-searchers leaving behind us a trail of wrappers and covers discarded as soon as we swallow the core. Training ourselves to see what lies hidden beneath the surface is discernment. Art helps us to see what otherwise we might never have noticed. Education in, to and by art is an essential nurturing of our humanity.

In general we would have to admit that we are careless about this aspect of our lives. Our history has been one of dereliction of duty in this area. It has not been entirely our own fault. Circumstances have militated against our sensual maturation. Nor has it helped that Ireland in the twentieth century, at the official level, was neglectful and suspicious of the arts. Artists and intellectuals were feared and suppressed by politicians, church leaders and society at large in a way that is both practically and symbolically expressed in the Censorship Act which was passed in 1929 and which held sway for about sixty years after that. Artists such as Yeats and Shaw did protest vehemently at the passing of this act at the time, and did manage to have the definition of 'indecent' as 'calculated to incite sexual passion' removed when they pointed out that this definition would deny Irish people access to most of the world's secular and religious art. However, the act went through and by 1930 every nude had been removed from the Municipal gallery, which was Ireland's leading gallery of 'modern' art at that time. Few artists felt welcome or safe to express themselves in any but the most traditional and righteous fashion.

Those who maintained the artistic tradition in this country in such oppressive circumstances were also subject to restricting parameters within their own domain. The Royal Hibernian Academy which directed things artistic and controlled the National College of Art was essentially conservative and maintained a romantic bias in favour of Irish academic realism centred mostly on landscape.

It was not until 1943 that Mainie Jellet, with Evie Hone and others, founded the Irish Exhibition of Living Art, partly out of frustration with the RHA which was rejecting works even by Louis le Brocquy, but also to introduce into Ireland the revolution in painting which had been energising the rest of the world for over half a century. Jellet had studied with Albert Gleizes, one of the first French advocates of non-representational painting. He was himself a painter, but more importantly he was an early theorist of cubism. His lectures of 1931–32 show that in his view cubism was a religious intuition concerning time and space. Far from being a revolutionary manifestation of esoteric progress, cubism was a return to a much more traditional type of art illustrated by details of Romanesque sculpture, for instance. Mainie Jellet was mainly responsible for whatever abstract and contemporary art began to emerge in the forties and fifties in Ireland.

In 1961 there was a Scandinavian report on design in Ireland which stated: 'The Irish schoolchild is visually and artistically among the most undereducated in Europe', an indictment re-echoed in 1965 by The Irish Council of Design which described education in this country as 'a tradition in which art as a whole has been gravely undervalued'. Over ten years later, after welcome reforms had been introduced into the education system, a report commissioned by The Arts Council of Ireland recognises that the 1970s were years of enlightened reform at every other level of the education system but 'the peripheral role which the arts have traditionally played in Irish Education has been perpetuated in the recent changes'. The same report warned that 'Ireland may be faced with a future public which, far from fruitfully exploiting the opportunities available to it, may be characterised by a uniform mediocrity of taste controlled by commercial interests'.[4]

What all this would mean for art in the religious life of the country is predictable enough. Philip Rice writing in the *Irish Spotlight* in 1966 talks about 'the hideous statues that clutter and defile our churches and make a mockery of the house of God', about 'ugliness, mediocrity', about 'ineptitude' which grossly dishonours God. 'Debased art-forms,' he suggests 'are harmful' because 'they dangerously distort the reality they stand for'. He concludes by admonishing: 'No more, please, of the refrain that this is what the people want'. However, he might be wrong there! It was, and is, to a large extent, what the people want, because they have never been shown anything else, or taught other ways of seeing. We have emerged after about a hundred years or more from a heritage of repository art which was sold internationally and cluttered our churches with what is known as kitsch, a German word for trash, meaning in this context mass-produced statues, pictures, ornaments, pastiche and plaster reproductions of classical models, which in their sentimental gaudy sameness are the antithesis of original works of art.

Milan Kundera has defined kitsch as 'the absolute denial of shit, in both the literal and the figurative senses of the word; kitsch excludes everything from its purview which is essentially unacceptable in human existence'. It is not so much its inherent ugliness which repels it is rather 'the mask of beauty it tries to wear':

> The feeling induced by kitsch must be a kind the multitude can share. Kitsch may not, therefore, depend on an unusual situation; it must derive from the basic images people have engraved in their memories. . . . Kitsch causes two tears to flow. The first tear says: How nice to see children running on the grass! The second tear says: How nice to be moved, together with all mankind, by children running on the grass!

What Kundera means by 'totalitarian' kitsch, where 'all answers are given in advance and preclude any questions', is a situation where everything that 'infringes on kitsch must be banished for life: every display of individualism (because deviation from the collective is a spit in the eye of the smiling brotherhood); every doubt, all irony (because in the realm of kitsch everything must be taken quite seriously).'[5]

Our Catholic cathedrals in this country are monuments to our imitative instincts and conservative distrust of artistic originality. After Catholic emancipation in 1829 when church building was once again a major industry and a dominant feature of every landscape in the country, two styles only seem to have been countenanced: the revival of Classic and Gothic architecture. The latter almost exclusively took over from about the middle of the nineteenth century.

It is therefore understandable that in 1949 when the building of the cathedral in Galway was commissioned it should have been conceived in a hybrid Romanesque style. That ten years later the foundation stone should have been laid and seven years later in 1965, that the Cathedral of Our Lady Assumed into Heaven and St Nicholas in Galway should have been dedicated, despite the fact that its architect had died before its completion, is one of the mysteries of human perversity and historical irony. It was in December of this same year that the Second Vatican Council of the Roman Catholic Church solemnly ended. Its revolutionary document, the Constitution on the Sacred Liturgy, which rendered the shape, style, arrangement and setting of such buildings obsolete and anachronistic had been promulgated two years previously. This building is almost an object lesson in the artistic insularity and myopic tenacity which accompanies the failure to educate our sensibilities. While the whole renewal of Vatican II was on the boil all over Europe and myriad manifestations of new and exciting trends in art and architecture were emerging on the continent of Europe, not just as fashionable displays of technical virtuosity but as genuine renewal of religious and theological awareness, the impoverished people of Galway were not just allowed but encouraged to erect, ironically and symbolically, on the site of a former prison, this gloomy monument in grey-green Galway limestone to our stubborn refusal to emerge from the empty tomb of medieval Christianity.

The late Michael Browne, the Bishop of Galway who had commissioned the cathedral and worked hand in hand with the architects, had left very explicit instructions even about each of the windows to be inserted into the walls of his design. Eight of these were installed in the 1960s, the remaining eighteen the year before the new millennium in 1999. There is a committee appointed, some of whom are relatives of the late bishop, who oversee the implementation of his dictated wishes in every detail: 'The stained glass windows in the Cathedral, are not merely to be decorative but to promote God's praise and glory by turning our minds devoutly towards God. The windows represent in vivid fashion the events of God's merciful dealings with his people and emphasise the importance of Scripture in the liturgy. All the windows depict biblical figures and events, those on the upper storey presenting the Old Testament while the windows on the ground floor depict events in the life of Our Lord.' The result of these, and other more particular stipulations for each individual window, has meant that the whole building seems to be studded with pages from an illustrated guide to the Hebrew and New Testaments. With some exceptions these are too literal, too figurative, too lack-lustre. There is an overwhelming mass of full length portraits, making the building feel like a waxwork museum: a 'who's who?' of the Bible.

Both James White, the late Irish historian and art critic, and Marie-Alain Couturier, the Dominican priest responsible in the fifties for the building of such beautiful and inspirational churches as those in Audincourt, Assy, Ronchamp and Vence, in which he commissioned the leading architects and painters of his generation such as Chagall, Matisse and Rouault, are agreed that 'to keep Christian art alive, every generation must appeal to its own masters of living art' as 'nothing is born or reborn except from life – not even tradition'. 'It is impossible,' says White 'to commission works of art under too precise instructions or requirements'. Obviously whoever is paying for it is permitted to give a detailed description of the kind of work they have in mind. However, 'there is no such thing as religious art, ecclesiastical art or liturgical art. These are merely terms denoting works of art, the subject matter of which puts them into special categories. Never before has art been more concerned with the spiritual than it is now'.[6]

It is clear from the late Bishop of Galway's instructions that for him art can be no more than decoration of his cathedral and illustration of either Scripture or a clearly formulated theology. Art is never imagined as an original source, as a spiritual revelation, as doing theology. It is clear why this situation of authoritarian penury should have come about. In the nineteenth century most of the leading painters and artists were free-thinking spirits who had little regard for the authorities of any of the churches and would never have been commissioned by those who were building cathedrals at the time. Instead they employed third-rate pious artists of no vision and less creativity to plaster or paint their ideologies on the inside of their equally obsolete buildings.

Bishop Browne has left explicit instructions about every detail of the amount and kind of art-work which should be commissioned to adorn his cathedral. A committee of loyal followers ensure that his instructions are followed as far as possible to the letter.

That is until you reach the recently installed James Scanlon windows. His recreation of the world in ultramarine blue with French glass that goes from black to white through every shade of blue and grey, begins the series. The set of six are high enough to see as one composition of movement, colour, tone, and shape, without getting trapped into the prescribed details. They also cover just one wall and are on their own without interference from other sources. The whole movie could be called: 'Sex, Violence and Chagall'. It is James Scanlon coming to terms with 'Our Dark Father', the God of our Irish Old Testament to whom Galway Cathedral is a sombre monument. After the creation of the world in ultramarine purity of blue, Adam and Eve enter the scene as unmistakable flesh. A tree, which structures the remaining windows, lavishly shelters them in its sensuous and colourful shade. This tree eventually whittles itself to a red skeleton in a black sky by the time we reach Abraham. In between there is the expulsion from Eden, flesh crawling towards the earth, and the ultramarine world sluiced with blood in the extraordinary window where Cain slaughters Abel. God's return burst of anger in the flood is stemmed by the colours of the rainbow. These windows depict our projection of nerves in patterns on the screen we call God. They are the Old Testament we have lived and then foisted on our maker. They are also a subversive manifesto: art is not a decorative illustration of what some theology might dutifully prescribe. Art is itself theology. And sometimes it has to burst an ecclesiastical eyeball to let the rainbow in.

Artists are not people with visions who belong to a world different from the one that we belong to. On the contrary, artists teach us how to live, move and have our being in this world, which, otherwise, we are inclined to misconstrue. In the sixties when liberation began to stir, and art as well as social life was influenced by a limited drug culture, people were suggesting that all kinds of visions were to be had as a result of certain 'hallucinating' substances. In his fascinating study of the effects of such habits, Aldous Huxley in his book *The Doors of Perception* produced a startlingly contrasting theory. His claim was that these drugs did not add anything to our normal vision. What they did was to remove the natural censorship and filtering system, which was like a customs and excise barrier around our visionary processes and which made us concentrate only on the data which would ensure our survival. According to him, each one of us is potentially 'Mind at Large', but to make survival possible 'Mind at Large has to be funnelled through the reducing valve of the brain and nervous system. What comes out at the other end is a measly trickle of the kind of consciousness which will help us to stay alive.' Most people, he claims, most of the time know only what comes through the reducing valve. The function of the brain, the nervous system and the senses is mainly eliminative, blotting out everything that is happening everywhere in the universe. We are protected from this surrounding mass of useless and irrelevant knowledge so we can concentrate upon 'that very small and special selection which is likely to be practically useful.' We are naturally equipped as eliminators of all that is not useful to us from our senses and our brains. However, Huxley continues, 'certain persons seem to be born with a kind of by-pass that circumvents the reducing valve. In others temporary by-passes may be acquired either spontaneously or as a result of deliberate "spiritual exercises" . . . through these permanent or temporary by-passes there flows not indeed the perception "of everything that is happening everywhere in the universe" (for the by-pass does not abolish the reducing valve, which still excludes the total content of Mind at Large), but something more than, and above all something different from, the carefully selected utilitarian material which our narrowed, individual minds regard as a complete, or at least sufficient, picture of reality.'[7]

So, when we talk about the connection between art and religion, the first possibility at the most basic level is clearance of vision. Art teaches us, or tries to teach us, how to see what is, rather than what is real for us. It tries to dispel the innate blindness of vision that religion also tries to dispel.

The Gospel of Mark Chapter 8 v 22f. gives the story of a miracle where Jesus cures a blind man. 'So He took him by the hand and led him outside the village. Then putting spittle in his eyes and laying His hands on him He asked, "Can you see anything?" And the man who was beginning to see replied: "I can see people like trees walking." And He laid his hands on the man's eyes again and he saw clearly . . . and he could see everything plainly and distinctly.' This account describes the

potential connection between religion and art. The way we see
'naturally' is distorted. Our normal vision is like a telescopic
lens on a gun; it fixes our sights on what we can gobble or grab.
Mostly we see people as we see trees in a forest. They mean
nothing to us. As we walk along a street, as we travel in a tube-
train, as we shuffle our way up a queue, people can be nothing
more than an unwelcome throng, a nuisance, a swarming
multitude, a faceless rabble. And yet each one of these is
potentially the most beautiful vision. It only requires that my
eyes be opened. This can happen, does happen, in the twinkling
of an eye. Suddenly the tree walking in front of me is
transformed into the most beautiful person I have ever seen in
my life. And then I see them as a loved one.

But strangely, what is required is not that my vision be
heightened or aggrandised but that it be smeared with reality,
that my eyes be bathed in spittle. Otherwise what I am looking
for and therefore looking at is likely to be not flesh and blood
reality but some idealised vision of my own imagining. Once I
accept that people are people and not gods or goddesses then
my attention can be focused. Otherwise it is irretrievably
attuned to another wave-length and the actual beauty of the
real world passes me by.

One of the great love stories of the world is *Anna Karenina*
by Leo Tolstoy. Anna and Vronsky are in love with each other
in a way and to a degree that has rarely been experienced or
articulated. They decide to let an unpleasant little Russian artist
living in Italy paint Anna's portrait.

> After the fifth sitting the portrait impressed everybody,
> especially Vronsky, not only by its likeness but also by its
> peculiar beauty. It was strange how Mihailov had been
> able to discover that peculiar beauty. 'One needs to know
> her and love her, as I have loved her, to discover the very

sweetest expression of her soul,' thought Vronsky, though it was only through this portrait that he himself learned this sweetest expression of her soul. But the expression was so true that it seemed to him, and to others, too, that they had always known it.[8]

It is not necessary to fall in love with people in order to see them as more than trees walking. Art can educate us to approach things as they are in themselves. Art can paint the portrait of things as they really are, can reveal to us 'the dearest freshness deep down things'. Art can help to open both us and the world around us to the dimension of the spirit, which is also the purpose of religion. In this way, some artists are prophets. Tolstoy tells us that even though Vronsky believed that he alone, as Anna's lover, could see the sweetest expression of her soul, it was only after the revelation of the artist that Vronsky and 'everybody' could really see what they thought they had always known.

Notes

1   Evemarie Schmitt, *Cézanne in Provence* (New York, Pegasus Library, Prestel, 1995), p. 92-3.
2   ibid., p. 73.
3   ibid., p. 98.
4   Ciarán Benson, *The place of the Arts in Irish Education*, Report of the Arts Council's Working Party on the Arts in Education (1979).
5   Milan Kundera, *The Unbearable Lightness of Being*, (London, Faber and Faber, 1984), pp. 248-52.
6   James White, 'Artists Role', *The Furrow*, 13.642, quoted in Richard Hurley, *Irish Church Architecture in the Era of Vatican II* (Dublin, Dominican Publications, 2001), pp. 107–8.
7   Aldous Huxley, *The Doors of Perception* (New York, 1970), pp. 22-4.
8   Leo Tolstoy, *Anna Karenina* (London, Penguin Classics, 1980), p. 503.

CHAPTER FOUR

Art and the Eucharist

CHRIST DOES NOT call us to a new cult which would be estranged from the normal rhythm of our lives, a new ritual gesture, a new devotion, a new prayer-machine. Christ calls us to life. Christianity is not a new religion, in some narrow sense of the word, it is a new form of existence. Nor is Christianity a new morality. It is a call to freedom – complete freedom.

The Christian is called forth (*Ecclesia*) by God to real freedom, real joy, real life, which are only possible in and through relationship with the only society of perfect love that has ever existed: the three persons in one God, the Trinity of perfectly equal and reciprocated love. Revelation of the Trinity is revelation to us of the meaning of 'person' as a reality, and the meaning of love, as a way of life and a way of being. These are not realities we can understand intellectually, they are realities which have to be done with the full reality of our total person and our whole life. Such is love as generosity, love out of plenitude not need, love as outgoing and selfgiving, an overflow of fullness. Prayer is allowing the life of the Trinity to circulate in our hearts. It is breathing the Spirit. We embody this love in such a way that it transforms us and we become its icons. The Spirit is the artist who moulds us into our most satisfying and appropriate shape which is in the image and likeness of God.

The Incarnation of Jesus Christ is the perfect translation of this perfect love into human terms. Exegesis means finding out what that means. Without encountering the details or weighing up the practicability, we are still aware that the very least it must involve are right relationships in every sphere. Everything that promotes fullness of humanity, that establishes relationships based on generous compassion furthers this cause. The second person of the Trinity became one of us to show all of us what we really are, or rather what we are capable of becoming. Christ became human to show us that real existence is quite different from what we had imagined. His life was a counterwitness to prevailing interpretations of the word 'life' and continues to be so.

The glory of God, as St Irenaeus has put it so succinctly, is any one of us fully alive, and 'orthodoxy' as the word tells us in Greek is exactly that: the right way to glorify God. Essential to that task is establishing real and lasting, indeed everlasting, contact with the living God. The ecstasy of God meets the ecstasy of human beings and this creates a new form of existence. This is not just rhetoric. Every person, whether divine or human is ecstatic. The very word 'existence' means to stand outside ourselves (*ex-sistere*). By nature our person is biologically incarnate in one limited, individual substance. Through love at even a human level we can escape from that imprisonment through ecstatic transport towards another human being. Eros is our self-transcendence, our going beyond the limits of our individual prison to be in communion with another. And even eros can further expand our transcendence of ourselves by becoming another human person. Just as each one of us is the product of love between two people, so our biological personhood achieves limited existence beyond our own span of life. Persons create other persons through erotic love. So the person in itself is capable of self-transcendence, self-perpetuation, even at the human level. What happens in the new form of life which God has allowed us to share is that our person becomes infixed in God's nature. This is what is meant by being adopted children of God. We cannot become such children naturally and so it has been arranged that we do so by adoption. Through the economy of the mystery our nature can then become interpenetrated by the divine properties of being. The ecstasy of our love can thereby become everlasting. The natural extinction of our bodily existence, when ingrafted to the body of Christ, is regenerated by an eternal energy which allows us to transcend the boundaries of our naturally limited personhood. The link between these two forms of personal life (ours and God's) is necessarily artificial, like an iron lung or a plastic limb; it is a new form of existence which we call 'ecclesial' (those who have been called out of their natural, biological, bodily individuality).

Our expression of that new form of existence is a new song, is praise. We are swept up into the love of God. Again, this phrase 'swept up' is not just a rhetorical and gushing form of hypnotic hyperbole. It is a new form of ecstatic existence. It is for real. God's love is contagious. But we must allow ourselves to be touched by it constantly to catch the fever. Sacramental life is providing those touchstones. This is what doing theology means. Anything less is heresy. Because heresy means cutting yourself away, cutting off the branch that holds you, or your nose to spite your face.

Orthodoxy moves our relationship beyond manipulation, using God or anyone else; beyond idolatry (about heaven), worshipping whatever or whoever enslaves us, holds us in thrall; beyond ideology (about earth), propaganda of whatever kind for whatever politics we hold. The possibilities we usually hope for are of our own invention, and we use worship as blackmail to force God's hand, to lure him into being implicated in our plans. This is religion and worship as politics or as investment. Worship as it should be means praise which is an attitude of openness and total trust in the future which God has opened for our attention and cooperation. We must not mortgage this future to buy what we want for the present. Instead we must be attentive to the slightest hint of possibility, perhaps only a whisper, undeveloped and unformed, which comprises a prompting by the Spirit. As we follow this hunch, what at first seems a barely audible whisper, eventually becomes ungainsayable and pivotal as a directive towards, or a burgeoning of, a quite different future to any we had ever imagined. We have no idea what life beyond the natural limitations of our being might look like, we have to be tutored in this as we have to be trained to walk the path of resurrection.

Such participation in the determination of a future as yet unimagined is the practical realisation of our frequent prayers, 'Thy kingdom come, Thy will be done'. It requires a concentrated orchestration of real presence to the present, to the moment which is the turnstyle towards the future. 'Religion,' says Rilke, 'is a natural animation within a being through whom the wind of God blows three times a day, as a consequence of which we are at least – supple'.[1] True worship as praise allows us to open fully as flowers do towards the sunlight, heliotropically, in the direction of the most expansive and fruitful future. It is the strange paradoxical condition of stubborn submission, conquering surrender. Such an exercise is open to the past through inspired *anamnesis*, remembering the wonderful working of God in our own lives as well as in the evolutionary impetus of the planet; and open to the future through *epiclesis* (invocation of the Spirit) which eliminates our own agenda and disposes us towards God's originality. In between the two movements towards past and future, comes the moment of consecration of the present, the platform from where we take our transport for that journey. Such real presence, as we call it, is accomplished in the Eucharist.

Every relationship requires rites, ceremonies, practical arrangements in time and space, to structure, maintain, fasten and secure the depth and durability of whatever we really want to hold on to, or whatever we are determined will come to pass. Christian liturgy has been called 'the cult of the Trinity': the way in which we accomplish in our space-time continuum the life of ever-expanding selflessness which is the invasion of our being by divine love.

Christianity as ritual must be anchored in the time and space of the original event of resurrected life. This is what we mean by apostolic tradition and this is also what we mean by humility. We are grounded in the real presence of the Risen Lord.

The essential connection between us and Divine life is not established, however, with and through the historical humanity of Jesus Christ as a man who shared our nature, it is established by with and through his person. As person he is one of the trinity of persons, he is self-giving communion with the other two persons, he is God as love. But, also as person, he is human and is in communion with each one of us to the extent that we realise this and live it with everything that we have and we are. Such is the essential business of Christianity. It is the business of love. Anything other than that, anything that distracts us from this essential relationship is leading us astray.

The Church and the Eucharist which establish the life of Christianity are instituted by Christ but constituted by the Holy Spirit.

Baptism, the Eucharist, the ecclesial community, establish our communion with the persons of the Trinity, energise our lives from eternity, burst through our space-time capsule and insert the oxygen of infinity, not just as an addition to, or a substitute for, our natural being, but as a transplant, a new creation, a relational metaphysics, a being as communion. What takes place is as miraculous and as revitalising as a heart transplant. Each one of us becomes energised by the heart of God.

The self-emptying of our being as autonomous, self-possessed, lonely individual substance, to allow for this transplant and the consequent harnessing of our human source of love to the infinite divine one, is the necessary preparation. Egotistical me can be corroded by the quicklime of the Eucharist, allowing me to become what I already am by baptism, an adopted member of this community of love. 'All our lives are the moment of Baptism' St Basil says. He means that it takes us that long to catch up with ourselves, to grow into the reality we have become by that mystery; growing into the reality of our new being, our everlasting life, our universal and eternal communion. We burst our being to get beyond it towards a new existence of love.

Real presence as the mystery of the Eucharist, in the mystery of the Eucharist. What does it mean? It cannot mean unrecognisably more than what we already know about being really present, otherwise it is beyond the spectrum of our capacity to know. If it means some kind of presence beyond all inkling of the kind of presence to which I am already accustomed in some way, it may work for angels or pure spirits or whatever, but it can't work for me. So the way to get a handle on it is to examine our own experience of real presence until it yields some insight into this other mystery which dares to speak its name.

Have you ever been really present to anyone else, to anything else? When during your day are you really present to yourself, when in all your life were you really present to anyone else? Most of us get up in the morning as automatons and many of us are not really present to anyone or anything, least of all ourselves, until lunchtime. There are exceptions but the problem is really yours not theirs – when are you awake, alive, present to being?

John Donne has a poem about being alive, being present for the first time. He calls it 'The Good-Morrow'. It tells his lover that until he met her he was fast asleep. So he says Good Morning to his waking soul for the first time in his life. Others describe five moments during their seventy-five years on earth when they were really present. Absenteeism from life is a major affliction of most on this planet. Some have to go to the North Pole, climb Mount Everest, land on the moon and then travel back to earth before they see it for the first time. Extreme, life-threatening situations make us present to ourselves and to the planet in ways that make our previous presence seem superficial.

On the morning of the 22nd of December 1849, Dostoevsky, who had been condemned to die, was led out to execution by firing squad. As the order to fire was about to be given he felt himself to be more alive and more present than ever before, since the day he was born. He saw with extraordinary lucidity the buttons on the jacket of the soldier who was facing him with a rifle and about to shoot. At that very dramatic moment a horseman rode into the courtyard with news of his last minute pardon. Dostoevsky made a vow from that moment onwards to live his life with the intensity and the presence he had experienced during that stay of execution. The movement we have nick-named 'existentialism' was one which promoted a similar intensity of real presence to the moment-by-moment ecstasy of existence. Philosophers of existentialism claim Dostoevsky as a founding father.

Most of us probably experience real presence when we are with someone we love. Even then it is difficult to find the times when both people are really present. We prepare the major moments with care. The atmosphere has to be right. The setting and the ritual have to be suitable. It doesn't just happen on its own. And even when all the preparations make everything perfect, there is no guarantee that we'll both be there really present to each other. If one of us has a toothache or is too tired or has received bad news; if the room is too cold, or I feel under pressure. The slightest thing can turn me off. Then I am not myself, or you are a hundred miles away, or we're both at one remove from each other. Perfect alignment of two presences happens once in a blue moon.

There are people who have a gift for such real presence. They can be there for most others whenever appropriate. That is also true for some great mystics. They can tune into the real presence of God, either by appropriate techniques they have learned, or by a genuine gift of prayer. However, Christianity is a democratic religion. It makes this presence available whether you or I are naturally gifted at being there or not.

The Church guarantees that Christ is 'really present' not just in some ethereal or 'spiritual' way but in his flesh and blood reality every time the mystery of the Eucharist is celebrated. This involves an adequate and valid celebration with all the constituent elements in working order, whether or not I am present either physically or psychologically. This is what is meant by the much maligned formula *ex opere operato*. It means that God will not renege on his promise to be there no matter how deficient the presence may be at the other side of the equation, namely our side. Whatever happens God will be there.

So, we have to establish what exactly is necessary for an adequate and valid celebration of the Eucharist before we try to describe what actually happens once those conditions are met. Two things are clear. Jesus Christ was the greatest religious and artistic genius who has ever existed and the work of art he produced as the Eucharist has survived him for over two thousand years.

The problems multiply when we try to establish what exactly he did and what we now need to do in order to re-enact it. Taking the complete panorama of evidence and reconstructing the original happening we seem to agree that the night before he died, Christ gathered his disciples around him and while they were having their evening meal he took bread, blessed it, broke it and gave it to his disciples saying: 'This is my Body'. Then in the same way, taking the cup of wine, he blessed it and gave it to them saying: 'This is my blood'. Then he further instructed them to 'Do this in memory of me'.

Later on of course, with hindsight and in retrospect, the disciples who were present and those who were not, began to read into this event all kinds of significance, most of which stemmed from the horrific outcome of that Thursday evening meal, when the celebrant was handed over to the authorities, tortured and crucified. It became clear that the actions he had performed the previous evening were ritual ones, whereby he was giving us his body and blood as a way of communicating with us beyond the reality of his impending death.

Later again, the followers of Christ realised that the meal during which Christ performed this extraordinary series of actions was in itself a Jewish liturgical celebration, a paschal meal, which was a ritual remembrance of the salvation of the Jewish people from the hands of their Egyptian masters, from slavery and subhuman existence.

An established liturgy emerged around the act of remembrance, and the various elements essential to a valid repetition of what the Lord had done were assembled and copperfastened into an established rite. Those of us who were born before 1960 will remember the Mass to which we in

Catholic Ireland had become beneficiaries. This rite was a legacy from the middle ages and its content and form were hammered into a monolithic structure in times of persecution, heresy, religious warfare and their corresponding attitudes of triumphalism, dogmatism, fanaticism. It seemed as if the Tridentine Mass (receiving its very name from the Council of Trent, which was summoned to elaborate the Catholic Counter-Reformation as an entrenched and defensive counter-attack against Protestantism) was the God-given ritual whereby Catholics were guaranteed to re-enact the presence of Christ in his body and blood as he was really present at the Last Supper.

This ritual was and is very splendid, very consoling, very mystical. It had and has enormous attraction for generations of practising Catholics. And yet, it was full of dangers and deceptions, not least of which were the devastating corollaries that this was the only way of salvation and that it was all that was necessary for salvation. It could become a magic formula to the point of superstition. The actual place where the bread and wine were changed into the body and blood of Christ became identified as the consecration. The priest uttered the magic formula and lo and behold (he raised the bread above his head) the deed was done. Priests became fetishistic, developed scrupulous fixations about saying the words distinctly in case the magic might not come through. Films were made and stories told about priests who uttered the magic words in brothels and restaurants, and about people who absconded with the magic particles to use their power in different circumstances for good or evil.

So, it was a good thing in some ways that the real presence of Christ in the Eucharist was definitively removed from any particular rite, from any particular set of objects and from any fixed verbal formulae. The Second Vatican Council reestablished the fact that the presence of Christ is both entirely free and gratuitous and is variously distributed in different ways and forms in the Eucharistic celebration, from the total assembly present, to the priest who is officiating in a ministerial capacity, to the word of Scripture spoken in the assembly, to the presence of the body and blood accomplished by the complete celebration of the Eucharistic prayer, which in itself can take on many forms and circumstances and be translated into any local language or set of cultural customs.

What happens on the altar when we celebrate the Eucharist is a mystery. But there are several approaches to mystery. We can treat it as a problem that has to be solved and can pursue it relentlessly until we have explained it adequately. Or we can abdicate all responsibility for making it accessible in any way, preferring that it remain totally incomprehensible and thereby even more mysterious, like the person who when asked what he thought about the mystery of three persons in one God, said he wished there were four of them so that he could believe in more of them. Mystery for the first category is like a mystery thriller, a detective story, you are kept guessing until eventually the secret is revealed and the mystery is solved. After that you lose interest and go on to the next one. You certainly don't go back over it again. The second approach is one of reverential awe and paralysed unworthiness. The mystery is mystery because I am so dull and unclean that it can have absolutely nothing to do with me. In between these extremes there is a middle way. The mystery was intended for me, has no function, reality or significance without me. Therefore unless I do everything in my power to prepare myself adequately and examine it as thoroughly as possible until it yields up to me something of its inherent splendour and its beneficial purpose in my regard, it could pass me by altogether without any impression or impingement.

There have been many attempts to 'explain' what happens during the Eucharist. Some of these make it sound like magic, others try to make it pass for science. Both approaches are understandable and natural. Most primitive tribes tried to harness the power of people they perceived as greater than themselves. Many believed that by eating the heart of a great warrior they would appropriate that energy or strength. This was probably the beginnings of a scientific rather than a magical mentality.

The middle ages made a brave attempt both to explain and to understand the mystery of what happens on the altar when the Eucharist is celebrated. They called it transubstantiation. This was the very brilliant and subtle attempt of Thomas Aquinas, among others, to translate the mystery into the most appropriate formulae of his time. Eventually the Church, even though hesitant and hostile at first, was so relieved and so impressed by the virtuosity and ingenuity of this succint explanation that it declared it to have been divinely inspired and from that time forward anyone who did not believe in transubstantiation would be a heretic.

Well there were all sorts of lessons in how to understand it and many suggestions about how to improve it. Transsignification and consubstantiation were proposed and rejected as inadequate and the word became something of a shibboleth and a defining war-cry, separating the sheep from the goats.

I am not saying that the explanation wasn't brilliant for its time; nor am I saying that it is an unworthy or inadequate vessel for transmitting the burden of the mystery. What I am saying is that no formula can capture the mystery and that this particular formula, although it may have been useful as a convenient holdall at a time when such a slogan was as necessary as it was inevitable, has outlived its usefulness and has become doubly unhelpful in the twenty-first century. I say doubly because it is betraying the whole notion of mystery which is much more important to inculcate into the contemporary religious sensibility, and because the whole philosophical framework within which it was originally enunciated has become obsolete. Scientific theory about matter over the last three hundred years is incapable of taking seriously an explanation of anything in terms of accidents and substantial forms. So, in order to sell the total package today one has to first of all give the faithful a crash course in one of the most sophisticated and complicated metaphysical systems ever enunciated, and then get them to apply this to the 'concrete' situation of the Eucharist.

Aristotle saw the things of this world as composite. They were made up of matter and form, which crudely speaking was explained to people as the way a sculptor takes a piece of rock or wood (raw matter) and puts a form on it, although in the full treatment of Aristotle it was more subtle and complicated than this. Apart from this distinction, another which defined everything in the world that is was the more difficult one of substance and accidents. Everything that is has a substance which could be described as 'an ultimate lump of stuff' which is the structure of its being, what underpins or undergirds (*sub-stare* = to stand underneath) it. Accidents are the other part of its composition and these are what we are able to apprehend with our senses. The volume, the shape, the size, the colour, the taste, the texture of anything is an accident. This is an unfortunate word because it means in philosophy something entirely different to what we normally think of when we hear the word. The car crash, the broken limb, the smashed tea-cup, the fall on ice: these are accidents in our vocabulary. For the inventors of the transubstantiation formula, accidents were all those things which accrued to a substance and which our senses were able to detect. What we could see, hear, touch, taste, smell of anything at all had to be an 'accident'. So, it was almost as if everything had two layers one substantial and the other accidental.

So, the first thing one had to do when explaining the 'mystery' of the Eucharist to anyone who wanted to be a Catholic was to give them the rules of the game they had to play. You explained to them about substance and accidents. You told them that everything they could see or touch or taste was an accident but that underneath these sensory data there was another reality which we call the substance. Then it was an easy move to explain what happened when we were celebrating the Eucharist. After the magic words of consecration when the priest (and it had to be an ordained priest, because anyone else would not have the power) had elevated the 'elements' of bread and wine, these particles of the created world were changed into the body and blood of Our Lord Jesus Christ. This happened, not at the level of accidents, which we could see or verify, it happened at the deeper level of substance to which no one had access. But if you were a Catholic you could 'see' with the eyes of faith that what was now on the altar was no longer the bread and wine but the body and the blood of Jesus Christ.

Now, Protestants and others who did not believe this were not really taking part in the Eucharist. Those of us who held to the doctrine of transubstantiation, however, were the real beneficiaries and the true inheritors of Christ's salvivic action and the life of grace.

Even as a child the first time this package was presented to me I found it phoney. Apart from the fact that contemporary physics had replaced the whole theory of substances with the more dynamic notion of atoms, molecules, neutrons, and electrons, which was just as implausible, just as mysterious, but which provided an equally convincing model for understanding. It suggested that the 'substantial' world we imagined was around us and which, indeed, we kept painfully bumping into, was in fact a deceptive bundle of evershifting particles which danced before our eyes like hoards of mosquitoes, masquerading as solid tables, chairs and other apparently substantial props within our domestic and neighbourhood scenarios. So, the two equally unconvincing 'explanations' at least had the effect of questioning the other's infallibility. Transubstantiation, even apart from the more modern competing explanation of the way 'things' are, had an inherent 'kings-new-clothes' atmosphere about it which begged too many questions.

I had been to a pantomime some time before the initation into the most secret mystery of my religion took place. One of the more far-fetched stunts of the comedian, mostly for the benefit of children, was to place two top hats on two chairs at either side of the stage. He explained that he was going to place an egg under one of these hats and by the pure power of his mental concentration he would move that egg from under the hat on the first chair right across the stage until it landed under the hat on the chair at the other side of the stage. He solemnly raised the hat and placed the egg underneath. He then marched to the centre of the stage and making appropriate gestures with his hands and screwing up his face into wrinkles of concentration while the orchestra played accompanying music descriptive of the movement, he 'conducted' the invisible egg from its position under the first hat to where he claimed to have landed it under the second one.

'Now children,' he told us pompously and condescendingly, 'the egg is under the second hat. Take my word for it.'

'Show us,' we screamed, 'lift up the hat.'

'Don't be impatient,' he said. 'Wait for the second part of the magic. I am now going to move that egg, with the pure power of my mental concentration, right back to where it came from under that first hat which you see over there.'

Amid storms of protest and howls of opprobrium, while the orchestra again obediently followed and illustrated both his deep concentration and the movement of the egg described unmistakably by his hands, he returned the 'substance' to the original place it had occupied.

'Now, children,' he said smugly as he lifted the hat for all of us to see, 'you can all see with your own eyes that the egg has returned safely to its original setting and all that happened through the power of the mind.'

There is no doubt that Aquinas had a different understanding from Aristotle of the substance/accident amalgam, infused as this was by his understanding of creation and of God as creator. Catherine Pickstock gives a contemporary account of this understanding in her book *After Writing* which has a very apposite subtitle from the point of view of this chapter: *On the Liturgical Consummation of Philosophy*. I shall summarise her interpretation, giving some of her own texts in the footnotes. In this context she understands Aquinas as saying that every particle of creation is, in fact, transubstantiated and that what happens in the Eucharist is only an extreme case of what happens all the time in terms of our existence here on earth.[2]

Just as the redness of a button on my coat can be 'substantial' in terms of the button, but 'accidental' in terms of the coat, so all creatures participate 'accidentally' in Being when placed in the context of God's creation although they may appear to be 'substantial' in themselves.

All bread is essentially 'accidental' in the sense that it derives its 'substance' from its being assimilated into bodies of one kind or another; it has no substantial reality in and for itself. As transubstantiated 'free-floating accidents' bread and wine can become 'directly sustained by their participation as particular contingent created things in the *esse* of the divinely transfigured human body to which they are conjoined'.[3] But in this they are simply repeating what has already happened from the beginning of time to every particle of creation through Christ, the Word, 'the lamb who has been slain since the beginning of the world'. (Rev 13:8)

The Eucharist also is Christ as he is and as he always has been from the beginning: as the fullness of everything and the only and inexhaustible source of life. In other words Christ has always been and always is nothing less and nothing other than the gift of the Eucharist, and the whole world in every possible particle of it is always potentially a Eucharistic element.[4] This point will be expressed in another way in the next chapter.

All of this suggests that the word 'transubstantiation', understood within the context of a metaphysics that is intellectually viable, can be used as a valid way of 'explaining' the mystery. However, it should not be imposed as an acceptable, still less as a prescribed, way of explaining the mystery which takes place in the Eucharist for people who have no initiation into the rarefied thought-forms which undergird its coherence. Such a metaphysical framework is really of little interest to people living in the twenty-first century and who hunger for the reality which the Eucharist has to offer. The twenty-first century must find its own way both of describing what is happening and of encouraging people to take part. No explanation is sufficient, no formula can capture the mystery, but the notion that we should cease from exploration and rely simply on an attempt made in the fourteenth century is both cowardly and suicidal. Cowardly because it shirks from the responsibility to promote; suicidal because such reliance on an obsolete explanation could ensure the demise of Eucharistic practice altogether.

The Gospel words are startlingly simple: Unless you eat my flesh and drink my blood you shall not have life in you. And the

night before he died Christ took bread, blessed it, broke it and
gave it to his disciples saying: This is my body. And taking the
wine he said: This is my blood. Do this in memory of me.
Many then left him because this was too hard a saying. When
the disciples questioned him and said do you mean this literally
or can we interpret what you have just said symbolically, he
more or less said take it or leave it – will you leave also?

How we explain this reality is a choice of language, of
images, of metaphors. In both the Scriptures and the early
Christian attempts to explain what happened, the way in which
God set out to give us his life, the mystery of our salvation
accomplished by, with and through Jesus Christ, myriad images
are used: pastoral imagery, Christ as the Good Shepherd;
military imagery, Christ as conqueror; medical imagery, Christ
as healer; sacerdotal imagery, Christ as high priest; sacrificial
imagery, Christ as lamb of sacrifice; and legal or juridical
imagery, Christ as redeemer (coming from the word as used
today for buying back what we have mortgaged). All of these
are attempts to explain a mystery; none of them have either a
monopoly or even pride of place.

So, we have the original event and now we have the present
circumstances. A ritual in which these words are repeated over
wine and a rather unrecognisable substitute for bread, and then
where the least likely of these is distributed to the congregation
and not the other, needs some vindication as replication either
of what happened or as what was intended. How did the
original gesture connect with the later 'sacrifice'of Christ, his
death on the cross, and how does the ceremony of today relate
to both these events?

A number of disconnected incidents or happenings may shed
some light and, at least help to excavate the extent of the problem.

In 1972 a rugby team was flying over the Andes mountains
when their plane crashed. Those who survived were stranded

without food or shelter on a snow-capped peak. Two of their teammates died in the crash. They had no means of communicating with the outside world and had no hope of being rescued. No-one knew of their whereabouts or realised that their plane had gone down. Eventually they were forced to cut up and eat the bodies of their dead friends. They described the horror and the difficulty which this decision caused and yet how they were driven to it by starvation and determination to survive. When eventually they were rescued and their story began to leak to the press, the whole world was appalled by this display of what was called cannibalism. The survivors were vilified as monsters and vampires. However, when these young and very ordinary people eventually appeared on television screens and told their story and when they said that this experience made them really understand what was meant by the words 'this is my body', which they had heard all their lives in terms of the Eucharist, then the public perception was altered and they became acceptable. So, the question is what could they have meant by that?

When you think of it, they must have meant exactly what some people believe when they are taking the Eucharist. In fact, when I was being prepared for Holy Communion in the 1950s I was told that I should never chew the host in case I might hurt our divine Lord by biting him. Also, a convert friend of mine says he became a Catholic because he had seen the blood in the chalice in a Catholic Church. And when we say that other denominations do not believe that the body of Christ is really present in the host are we not saying that they do not have the actual limbs in their mouths.

Such a literal translation has been condemned by the Church and those who gave grisly descriptions of how they were chewing muscle and sinew were declared to be heretics or insane. So, let's face it – we are not saying that.

On the other hand, we are not saying that the bread and the wine are simply replacing the body and blood either as symbols (transsignification) or as capsules (consubstantiation), we are insisting that in between these two possibilities, eating flesh as a cannibal eats flesh and eating bread as a meat substitute which can also act as a reminder of what someone wonderful did for us, there is a third – and this is what we call the 'sacramental' reality. Now, we do have to acknowledge that the word is the Latin translation for 'mystery'. And so we are back again where we started: we are using a mystery to express a mystery.

However, two examples of such 'sacramental' presence in everyday experience may help to unravel something of the second mystery.

When we go to a play, there is a space and time on the stage while the play is in progress which is not the space and time we engage with in the foyer, the auditorium before the lights are dimmed, or when we go out onto the street. While the play is in progress there is a space which is demarcated and which is inhabited by the actors in such a way that it leaves me as a member of the audience definitively outside. Even if I were to leave my seat, walk onto the stage and sit down beside one of the actors or actresses, even hug them close to me, I would still not be a part of the space they are in. I could be as close to any of these actors as is possible, closer in terms of proximity than any of them is to each other and still I would not be part of their world. In fact, the Greeks had two words for space which underscored these two dimensions: *Topos* and *Chora*. Our words topography and topology help us to see the difference, the latter being a mathematical term for the study of geometrical properties and spatial relations unaffected by continuous change of shape or size of figures. In his play, *Translations*, Brian Friel describes Ireland as a country in terms of pure geography which can be measured and assessed on an ordinance survey map (topography) and also, from another point of view, as a sacred place known only to the inhabitants who understand the names of each locality. In ancient Greek theatre, mediation between the space of the theatre and the space of the auditorium, to which we return when the magic of the play has been terminated, was the role of the chorus, which word came from the same root as *chora*, the second kind of space. Here you can travel in time and imagination and land yourself in another country at another time, another century, within the time-capsule of the current clock of your chronological life.

At a spatial level the example of the old boots which Van Gogh painted and which now hang in various museums around the world may help. The boots are there on the wall in New York and hopefully will be there for at least a hundred years more. The actual shoes which were painted in Provence a hundred years ago have long since disappeared. Their reality, their memory, their existence live on in a very particular and yet recognisable way in the time-space sacrament of art.

Every single element of the Eucharistic rite is artistic in the sense that it occurs because someone decided that it should. These decisions may have been made in the light of some divine revelation or as some previously performed action of a divine person, but their actual presence and their performance or the way they either appear or are articulated, all derive from the work of human hands. From the moment we begin the ceremony, the way we begin, the way we process, the clothes, garments, robes we wear, the chants we sing, the candles, incense, insignia, accompanying officials, to the building we use, the elements of the celebration, the altar, the disposition of the participants, the placing of the acoutrements, the altar linens, the cruets, the patens, chalices, books, the accompanying music, the rubrics of how and when we stand, sit, kneel, prostrate ourselves, enter or exit, and so on. Every single one of these derives from some historical culture, depends upon some theological interpretation, results from some human decision about its appropriateness and its necessity for conducting the rite.

On the other hand, each one of these elements, actions, words, gestures, garments, implements, containers and paraphernalia should be examined constantly and replaced or removed wherever they are found to be mere quirks of human idiosyncracy or stubbornness. This applies more urgently to elements and additions which accrued from cultures and ages which were demeaning or disrespectful towards certain members of the congregation who might have been discriminated against for their race their sex or their class. Any element of the Eucharistic ceremonial which fails to promote the dignity of the human person, the cultivation of the real presence of both the living God and every member of the participating congregation, which denotes any whisper of exclusivity, should be removed.

What Christ did was to give us his body and blood. This makes us partakers of his divinity, makes us lovers of his calibre, makes us alive in the way that he was alive, which means as resurrected bodies. He did this by taking elements of our created world, the ones that were to hand for an ordinary meal, the ones we constantly and regularly use to nourish the very bodies that he was trying to raise from the dead. These happened to be bread and wine because of the cultural circumstances in which the original meal took place.

However, there was never meant to have been some kind of fetishistic obsession with these random foodstuffs. The notion that cultures who never drink wine and have never eaten bread should import these in order to have a valid Eucharist is humanly perverse. Also, the elements which Christ used were meant to be bodily, physical, material elements. The way in which we have tried to remove their physicality, their materiality, by turning the bread into barely visible or tangible hosts of unleavened bread of angels (*Panis Angelicus*) which can melt into our tongues without any effort to chew, is the result of a cultural proclivity, not to say perversity, which should be abandoned wherever this seems reasonable or desirable; it can also be maintained wherever the sensibilities of believers have become accustomed or attuned to such refinement. The important point is that it doesn't matter which kind of element one uses, the reality is that Christ has become incarnate in our natural world and that, as Teilhard de Chardin so vividly perceived and described, this means that the body of Christ has become transubstantiated within the evolutionary process of the universe also through these participating elements until Christ becomes all in all.

In the next chapter I use the work of one priest-poet whose life was spent examining these mysteries and who, in my view, succeeded in developing the doctrine of the Eucharist to include much more than our restricted understanding had seen or imagined.

Notes

1 Rainer Maria Rilke, *Selected Letters* (London, Quartet Books, 1988), pp. 336-7.

2 'Hence every creature is "pulled" by its participation in *esse* beyond its own peculiar essence – it exceeds itself by receiving existence – and no created "substance" is truly substantial, truly self-sufficient, absolutely stable or self-sustaining. It follows that the violation of the substance/accident contrast and the gap between *esse* and essence in the case of transubstantiation is only an extreme case of what, for Aquinas, always applies. All substances are "accidents" in contrast to divinity, and become signs which, in their essence, realize a repetition

and revelation of the divine "substance" (although Aquinas finds even the category of "substance" to be inadequate for God).' Catherine Pickstock, *After Writing: On the Liturgical Consummation of Philosophy*, (Oxford, Blackwell, 1999), p. 260-1.

3 Ibid., p. 260

4 'If the Eucharist repeats what was in the first place a repetition, then it repeats Christ as Himself always nothing other than the gift of the Eucharist. This Christology is most fully expressed in St John's Gospel, whose prologue was often recited at the Last Gospel, by the Priest and Ministers during their recession or unvesting at the end of the Mass in the medieval Roman liturgy.

In this Gospel, the Logos is described as *plemora* – that is, as fullness, an inexhaustible source of life. He is at once everything and more than everything, and yet, in the Johannine story, he is present through testimony and supplementation. Paradoxically, Jesus is the fulfillment of all signs, and yet is only revealed through a series of signs.' Ibid., p. 264-5

CHAPTER FIVE

Hopkins Between
Two Wrecks

THERE IS A quantum leap in the poetry of Gerard Manley Hopkins between what he wrote before 1875 and what he wrote after that year, which critics have explained variously from excoriated sensuousness to manic depression of a cyclothymic kind.[1] Whatever the causes the results are stylistic genius. The causes nearly always appear in literary criticism as biographical or psychological. There seems to be little doubt that Hopkins turned into a poetic genius around this time. The poetry he wrote before 'The Wreck of the Deutschland' would not have won for him the place he now holds in English literature. It seems also true to say that for most of his life Hopkins was what might be described as a psycho-sexual mess. Does one of these realities throw light upon, or explain the other? I am sure they do, and there have been convincing attempts to make the second half of such an equation into a comprehensive explanation of the first.

The purpose of this chapter is to suggest that one major element in the poetic genius of Hopkins is an inspiration that lies outside such psychological and biographical circumstances and which has left a recognisable and identifiable stamp on his work. This is the life and energy of the three persons of the Triune God to whom, at a very early age, he gave himself, and who accepted this invitation and permeated his life and his work with precisely the hallmark that now makes Hopkins one of the forerunners of contemporary verse and one of the lasting voices among a plethora of his coevals who imagined themselves to be more significant than he. The few who were privy to his poetic experimentation seem to have regarded him as a quaint and convoluted dabbler in an art form which was beyond him.

The way to prove, or rather to manifest, this hypothesis is, of course, to show the footprints, the watermark of the Trinity in the text, which I hope to do. It must be clear to anyone with any knowledge of Hopkins the human being that whatever about his desire to be a poet, to be famous, to be fruitful, and whatever about possible suppressed yearnings for friendship, for freedom, for erotic stimulation, his deepest, most genuine and life-long desire was for union with God. And, my contention is that just as other similarly haunted individuals ended up with bodily manifestations of their overriding and obsessive impetus, the poetry of Hopkins has been similarly marked and energised in ways that explain the seismic shift between its earlier and later manifestations.

Hopkins wrote 'The Wreck of the Deutschland' in December 1875. Writing to R.W. Dixon (5 October 1878) he tells him about his poetry:

> You ask, do I write verses myself. What I had written I burnt before I became a Jesuit and resolved to write no more, as not belonging to my profession, unless it were by the wish of my superiors; so for seven years I wrote nothing but two or three little presentation pieces which occasion called for. But when in the winter of '75 the *Deutschland* was wrecked in the mouth of the Thames and five Franciscan nuns, exiles from Germany by the

Falck Laws, aboard her were drowned I was affected by the account and happening to say so to my rector he said that he wished someone would write a poem on the subject. On that hint I set to work and, though my hand was out at first, produced one. I had long had haunting my ear the echo of a new rhythm which I now realised on paper.[2]

The occasion of this poem released Hopkins from his self-imposed silence and he wrote poems from then until his death. However, he was never quite happy that the 'permission' he had received for this one poem could be extended legitimately to all the later ones he wrote. Again writing to Dixon (2 November 1881):

The question then for me is not whether I am willing (if I may guess what is in your mind) to make a sacrifice of hopes of fame (let us suppose), but whether I am not to undergo a severe judgement from God . . . for the waste of time the very compositions you admire may have caused and their preoccupation of the mind which belonged to more sacred or more binding duties, for the disquiet and the thoughts of vainglory they have given rise to. A purpose may look smooth and perfect from without but be frayed and faltering from within. I have never wavered in my vocation, but I have not lived up to it. I destroyed the verse I had written when I entered the Society and meant to write no more; the *Deutschland* I began after a long interval at the chance suggestion of my superior, but that being done it is a question whether I did well to write anything else. However, I shall, in my present mind, continue to compose, as occasion shall fairly allow, which I am afraid will be seldom and indeed for some years past has been scarcely ever, and let what I produce wait and take its chance; for a very spiritual man once told me that with things like composition the best sacrifice was not to destroy one's work but to leave it entirely to be disposed of by obedience.

Hopkins believed in the poem he had written under obedience. Against hostile criticism from his friend the poet Robert Bridges he holds firm in a letter (21 August 1877): 'I cannot think of altering anything.' The poem is a gift, a grace. He agrees that it is obscure and intended as such (13 May 1878): 'Granted that it needs study and is obscure, for indeed I was not over-desirous that the meaning of all should be quite clear.' He also agrees with Bridges (Letter of 2 April 1878) that as a narrative poem about the wreck of a ship carrying five nuns from Germany, it is unwarrantedly complicated:

> The *Deutschland* would be more generally interesting if there were more wreck and less discourse, I know, but still it is an ode and not primarily a narrative. There is some narrative in Pindar but the principal business is lyrical. This poem on the Eurydice is hitherto almost all narrative however.

So, between the writing of 'The Wreck of the Deutschland' and the writing of 'The Loss of the Eurydice', which were ostensibly poems about similar events, Hopkins had regained control of his poetry, and the second poem is a narrative about a shipwreck, which the first had refused to be. It is as if Hopkins was writing the second poem under the guidance of critics like Bridges in something of the way his second-last sonnet to 'RB' is almost an exercise in sonneteering in the manner prescribed by his friend, who at the time was a much more important poet than he.

Something else happened in the *Deutschland* poem that made it an ode rather than a ballad; more lyrical than narrative and more favoured by Hopkins himself, almost because it had somehow escaped his mastery and was an unruly firstborn. Writing to Dixon (29 March 1879) he admits that 'the *Deutschland*, earlier written, has more variety but less mastery of the rhythm', and to Bridges (26 January 1881) he agrees 'that the Eurydice shews more mastery in art, still I think the best lines in the "Deutschland" are better than the best in the other. One may be biassed in favour of one's firstborn though'. With hindsight and at our distance from those dates over a century later, it is so clear that Hopkins is right and that Bridges was an unhelpful and discouraging critic of his more original but diffident friend.

So, what is in the first wreck that isn't in the second? What is in the 'Deutschland' that is more than mere narrative? The first thing is the 'new rhythm' whose echo had long been 'haunting' his ear and which the occasion of the wreck allowed to become poetry; the second is Hopkins himself. In that same letter (21 August 1877), in which he vigorously defends 'the *Deutschland* on her first run' he confides to Bridges 'that what refers to myself in the poem is all strictly and literally true and did all occur; nothing is added for poetical padding'.

There are two prevalent accounts of this story of the sensitive, scrupulous, somewhat neurotic Hopkins torn between two vocations. On the one hand there are those who decry the artistic abortion that Jesuit life performed on the young aspirant to the priesthood. Just as the Jesuits would later cauterise the boy poet, James Joyce, by their harsh treatment of the artist as a young man, so their beliefs, fanaticism, anti-artistic lifestyle, and obediential strait-jacket, lost for literature a poet as prolific and as naturally gifted as Keats.

The other view is that Hopkins might have been a second-rate Victorian poet in the manner of Swinbourne or Rossetti if he had not undergone the acid bath of Roman Catholicism and Jesuit discipline. One commentator elegantly derides that part of the 'Deutschland' which came to Hopkins first, the narrative verses: 'we fear lest the tall nun riding the storm be dragged anapestically in the wake of Paul Revere . . . dangerously descending the rhythmic path of Longfellow.'

The purists of this second school would hold that the full significance and architectonic structure of the poem is to be found in the Roman Catholic beliefs and doctrines that imbued the life and consciousness of Hopkins from the time of his conversion. These can be found in his sermons, devotional writings, journals and letters. In other words, they would hold that Hopkins was saved from weaker, more sentimental, romantic poetry by the Roman Catholic Church, and his greatest poetry, the vehicle of his genius, is Roman Catholic poetry.

The point of view that I now propose is somewhere between these options, between the two wrecks. My claim is that there is a further element in the fashioning of the poetic genius of Hopkins. All his talk about obedience and permission to write poetry is ambiguous. The occasion of the wreck itself and the hint given by his superior, were no more than alibis for that 'echo of a new rhythm' that had been 'long haunting' his ear, to emerge and get itself down on paper. Hopkins himself may have been duped by these subtle ruses of the poetry and the language that longed to hear itself. He began to write a narrative poem about the nuns who were martyred and did manage to end up with a plea for the conversion of England, but, fortunately, this tedious voyage, which could have been as banal as the later one on the Eurydice, underwent its own particular wreck which instigated the flowering of the poetic genius of Hopkins and his entrapment in the history of literature.

So, putting it simply, I would agree that Hopkins was saved from an inferior, predictable, romantic poetry by the Roman

Catholic church; but in a further and more crucial step, he was saved by poetry and language itself from a maudlin triumphalist Roman Catholicism which is everywhere irritatingly present in his prose and more self-conscious poetry. And, I say more: the subtle revolt that led to 'The Wreck' (Hopkins himself frequently refers to his two poems as 'my wrecks') turned him into a poetic Trojan horse within the walls of Catholicism, within the very bastion of Jesuitry. The Catholicism that saved him from 'poesy' and the poetry that saved him from Catholicism combined to institute through him a revolution. The genius of Hopkins joined the two traditions of English literature and Roman Catholicism, but both traditions underwent salvific osmosis in the work achieved by his originality. There was more than one wreck in 1875: the most felicitous one was the neurotic, self-destructive Catholic piety of the author.

To back up this proposal I want to examine the moment of 'inspiration' that initiated the first poem Hopkins had written for seven years and the workings of what he called his 'Muse', without whose fickle, rare but overwhelming visits he was unable to write any poetry; also to find in the poem itself evidence for the revolution of the word which 'The Wreck of the Deutschland' initiated. In a letter to Bridges (13 May 1878) Hopkins recognises its originality: 'When a new thing, such as my ventures in the *Deutschland* are, is presented us, our first criticisms are not our truest, best, most homefelt, or most lasting.' Although advised by Bridges to alter some of it, Hopkins felt he had no right to change anything in it because it was given to him by a force of inspiration outside himself. Again in a letter to Bridges (2 April 1878): 'My muse turned utterly sullen in the Sheffield smoke-ridden air and I had not written a line till the foundering of the Eurydice the other day and that worked on me and I am making a poem – in my own rhythm.' Later in a letter (16 September 1881) describing the ode he hoped to write to Edmund Campion, he says:

> Thinking over this matter my vein began to flow and I have by me a few scattered stanzas, something between the *Deutschland* and *Alexander's Feast*, in sprung rhythm of irregular metre. But the vein urged by any country sight or feeling of freedom or leisure (you cannot tell what a slavery of mind and heart it is to live my life in a great town) soon dried and I do not know if I can coax it to run again. One night, as I lay awake in a fevered state, I had some glowing thoughts and lines, but I did not put them down and I fear they may fade to little or nothing.

The impetus that prompted the muse on both these occasions was 'shipwreck'. Something about shipwreck coaxed the vein of poetry to run. Writing to his mother (Christmas Eve 1875) he thanks her for sending him accounts from the newspapers, but he reprimands her because she 'omitted the most interesting piece of all, the account of the actual shipwreck: fortunately I had read it but still I should have been glad to have it by me to refer to again, for I am writing something on this wreck, which may perhaps appear but it depends on how I am speeded. It made a deep impression on me, more than any other wreck or accident I ever read of.'

It is true that Victorians seem to have been obsessed by wrecks. The move from slow-moving country life to the machine age, from the natural to the mechanical, caused much nostalgia and misgiving. The new-fangled machines seemed like monsters and when they crashed or sank it was so calamitous that it almost painted itself as retributive justice for having made them in the first place. There is something of the voyeur's *frisson* in the multiplicity of paintings and descriptions of such wrecks in the art and journalism of the time. That the vein of Hopkins' major poetry was touched by such disasters at sea can be explained by two quotations from his prose writings. The first describes a day during the Long Retreat which ended on Christmas Day, when Hopkins suddenly began to cry and sob in the refectory while the account by Sister Emmerich of the Agony in the Garden was being read aloud (Journals: 23 December 1869):

> I suddenly began to cry and sob and could not stop. I put it down for this reason, that if I had been asked a minute beforehand I should have said that nothing of the sort was going to happen and even when it did I stood in a manner wondering at myself not seeing in my reason the traces of an adequate cause for such strong emotion. . . . But neither the weight nor the stress of sorrow, that is to say of the thing which should cause sorrow, by themselves move us or bring the tears as a sharp knife does not cut for being pressed as long as it is pressed without any shaking of the hand but there is always one touch, something striking sideways and unlooked for, which . . . undoes resistance and pierces, and this may be so delicate that the pathos seems to have gone directly to the body and cleared the understanding in its passage. On the other hand the pathetic touch by itself, as in dramatic pathos, will only draw slight tears if its matter is not important or not of import to us, the strong emotion coming from a force which was gathered before it was discharged.[3]

The 'strong emotion coming from a force which was gathered before it was discharged' in 'The Wreck of the Deutschland', and which was triggered by the tangential and unlooked-for account of the actual wreck, was the deeply pressing knife, the

weight and stress of that which is the source of all poetry. As
Hopkins wrote to Bridges (15 February 1879):

> I cannot in conscience spend time on poetry, neither have
> I the inducements and inspirations that make others
> compose. Feeling, love in particular, is the great moving
> power and spring of verse and the only person that I am
> in love with seldom, especially now, stirs my heart
> sensibly and when he does I cannot always 'make capital'
> of it, it would be sacrilege to do so.

The implication is that Christ did stir Hopkins' heart on the one
occasion at least where he was sure the motivation to write was
divinely inspired. The wreck was the occasion for that well of
feeling and emotion to emerge in the haunting rhythms that
had pursued him long before. The poem that sprang forth was
meant to be a narrative sermon for the conversion of England.

The poem is neither a narrative nor a sermon. It is an ode, a
lyric, a love-poem. It describes the 'lovescape' of Christianity as
this had been experienced by Hopkins in his relationship with
'the only person' with whom he was in love. And this love beats
down, presses down on him and causes in him the stress and
emotion that the image of the wreck helps him to recognise as
a sensation of drowning. In his journal, he describes a
nightmare he had, which was about such pressures (18
September 1874):

> I had a nightmare that night. I thought something or
> someone leapt onto me and held me quite fast: this I
> think woke me, so that after this I shall have had the use
> of reason. This first start is, I think, a nervous collapse of
> the same sort as when one is very tired and holding
> oneself at stress not to sleep yet suddenly goes slack and

seems to fall and wakes, only on a greater scale and with a loss of muscular control reaching more or less deep; this one to the chest and not further, so that I could speak, whispering at first, then louder – for the chest is the first and greatest centre of motion and action, the seat of Thumos. I had lost all muscular stress elsewhere but not sensitive, feeling where each limb lay and thinking that I could recover myself if I could move my finger, I said, and then the arm and so the whole body. The feeling is terrible: the body no longer swayed as a piece by the nervous and muscular instress seems to fall in and hang like a dead weight on the chest. I cried on the holy name and by degrees recovered myself as I thought to do. It made me think that this was how the souls in hell would be imprisoned in their bodies as in prisons and what St Theresa says of the 'little press in the wall' where she felt herself to be in her vision.

The first part of 'The Wreck of the Deutschland', written after the narrative proper in the second part, parallels the sonnet 'written in blood' in 1885, ten years later, called 'Carrion Comfort', where 'love' is described as a wrestling match between God and the poet. Here the 'wreck' is used as the image to convey the 'lovescape' of divine providence both as it occurred in Hopkins' personal experience and in the incarnational pattern of the Trinitarian mystery.

Christ as wrestling lover is present in the shipwreck, just as he was present, even though asleep, in the storm experienced by his disciples:

> Then he got into the boat followed by his disciples. Without warning a storm broke over the lake, so violent that the waves were breaking right over the boat. But he was asleep. So they went to him and woke him saying,

'Save us, Lord, we are going down!' And he said to them, 'Why are you so frightened, you men of little faith?' And with that he stood up and rebuked the winds and the sea; and all was calm again. The men were astounded and said, 'Whatever kind of man is this? Even the winds and the sea obey him.'(Matthew 8: 23–27)

Hopkins refers specifically to this passage when he is identifying himself in his mystical struggle with the tall nun who perished on the *Deutschland*. Her attitude was different from that of the apostles: 'They were else-minded then, altogether, the men/ Woke thee with a *We are perishing in* the weather of Gennesareth.' She, when she called out 'O Christ, Christ, come quickly' was not uttering the same faithless sentiments, rather she – in Hopkins' beautiful but strange phrase – 'christens her wild-worst Best'. This is exactly what Hopkins himself was doing in those so-called 'terrible' sonnets of his later years. 'What did she mean?' he asks himself.

Breathe, arch and original Breath.
Is it love in her of the being as her lover had been?
Breathe, body of lovely Death.

Or, in a third hypothesis, he asks himself, was she asking for a quick end to this struggle so that she might enter the peace and fulfilment of her heavenly reward? In verse 27 he is quite clear that none of these three possibilities provides an answer to the ecstatic call of the tall nun: 'O Christ, Christ, come quickly.' He first of all chides himself on his presumption to superimpose his own experience on dry land, as it were, with 'her mind's/ Burden, in wind's burly and beat of endragoned seas.' But then he overcomes that scruple in wonderful lines of tentative acknowledgement of the strength and power of his own experience of such love introduced by the Incarnation, which culminated in the Crucifixion, which then exploded into the ecstasy of Resurrection, as a bodily act. To understand this act, the nearest approximation and analogy we have at our disposal is the sexual act. Such a reality is articulated musically in various stanzas of 'The Wreck of the Deutschland':

> But how shall I . . . make me room there:
> reach me a . . . Fancy, come faster –
> Strike you the sight of it? look at it loom there,
> Thing that she . . . There then! the Master,
> Ipse, the only one, Christ, King, Head:
> He was to cure the extremity where he had cast her;
> Do, deal, lord it with living and dead;
> Let him ride, her pride, in his triumph, despatch and have
>   done with
> his doom there.

> Ah! there was a heart right!
> There was single eye!
> Read the unshapeable shock night
> And knew the who and the why; . . .

> Jesu, heart's light,
> Jesu, Maid's son,
> What was the feast followed the night
> Thou hadst glory of this nun?

Relationship with God has often been described in sexual imagery, from the many passages in the Old Testament, whether in Jeremiah, Ezechiel, or the Song of Songs. It has been a constant theme of mystics in every religious tradition. Everything about the Crucifixion of Christ's body: the scourging, piercing, crowning with thorns, driving in of nails, has a connotation of penetration. It is a searching out, as psalm 138 puts it: 'My body held no secret from you.' The psalm spoken by Christ on the cross (Psalm 21) describes how 'they tear holes in my hands and my feet' and asks to be delivered from 'the horns of these oxen'. It is another way of depicting the 'lovescape' of divine penetration: crucifixion as breaking and piercing the body to allow divine love to break through.

In Hopkins' poetry there are images of various kinds of torture that transform one substance into another: the way wine or oil are made, for instance, out of crushed grapes or olives. The Crucifixion, which produced in Christ's body the glory that flames out 'like shining from shook foil' or gathers 'to a greatness like the ooze of oil/ Crushed'. And in a lesser poem, 'Barnfloor and Winepress', he makes the explicit connection between the bread of the Eucharist, 'scourged upon the threshing floor', and the wine 'racked from the press', and the crucified body of Christ.

It is as if the violent death of crucifixion or of shipwreck and drowning were a kind of rape.

It is to celebrate and express this kind of loving that the poem is given. But it is not just the Crucifixion of Christ that provides the shape, the stress and the archetype of Christian sacrificial love. This was the great truth that Hopkins gleaned from the thirteenth-century Scottish theologian, Duns Scotus: the Incarnation was the inscape of the Word from the beginning of time, not just when Christ came on earth. Incarnation was a reality from the beginning of time and the lamb, who was slain since the beginning of the world, as the book of the Apocalypse puts it, is present in every natural manifestation of this adventure of love. So that the 'stress' of incarnation 'rides time like riding a river' and is everywhere 'a stress that stars and storms deliver' to anyone who can see and understand it. The perfection of such sacrificial love was indeed achieved by Christ on earth through his passion and death as verse seven of 'The Wreck of the Deutschland' explains:

> It dates from day
> of his going in Galilee;
> Warm-laid grave of womb-like grey;
> Manger, maiden's knee;
> The dense and the driven Passion, and frightful sweat;
> Thence the discharge of it, there its swelling to be,
> Though felt before, though in high flood yet –
> What none would have known of it, only the heart,
>   being hard at bay,
>
> Is out with it! Oh,
> We lash with the best or worst
> Word last! How a lush-kept plush-capped sloe
> Will, mouthed to flesh-burst,
> Gush! – flush the man, the being with it, sour or sweet,
> Brim, in a flash, full! – Hither then, last or first,
> To hero of Calvary, Christ,' feet–
> Never ask if meaning it, wanting it, warned of it – men
>   go.

Christ underwent crucifixion and death for our participation in the same mystery in our own way, whether willingly or reluctantly, whether knowingly or unaware. Hopkins takes the insight of Scotus and turns it into an original expression of the Christian mystery. Flood, storm, shipwreck, can all be powerful and poignant icons of sacrifice, or sacraments of love, as crucifixion can be. One of the great Roman Catholic theologians of the twentieth century, Hans Urs Von Balthasar, who was also a Jesuit for a time, uses Hopkins as one of the major studies in his Magnum Opus on theological aesthetics and is almost shockingly explicit in this sense:[4] 'In the great shipwreck poem, man is the succulent fruit that God bites in order to know its innermost taste, and in being this fruit for God, mankind treads, willy-nilly, the way to Calvary'. He then quotes the famous lines about the 'lush-kept plush-capped sloe' which is 'mouthed to flesh-burst' and he elaborates:

> This doctrine of grace changed the natural doctrine of instress and inscape, for the true inscape of all things is Christ; God's grace is the stress within them . . . For now it is really God who has the true taste of the human self in his mouth.

Lastly, riding the intuition of Scotus and following his own inspiration again, Hopkins 'whirled out wings that spell' yet another kind of 'lovescape' which is the writing of the poem itself. Both the reading and the writing of this poem require a kind of submission to the rhythm which is similar to the surrender to the sea.

And the poem was given, or rather, it came through the wreck of Hopkins' priestly vocation, in a sense. The vows of chastity and obedience were the most difficult for him. He managed to circumvent the second through the hint given by his superior, but he was haunted all his life by his 'unchaste' nature. He was aware how prone he was to thoughts of a sexual kind which were mostly aroused in him by male bodies but also sometimes by horses and other beautifully sleek-skinned animals. He knew that certain paintings and certain people gave him disturbing sexual fantasies, and he was aware that there was no human being more temperamentally akin to himself than Walt Whitman, whose poetry, from the Hopkins perspective, indulged to the full the freedom and lasciviousness of homoerotic impulse. Hopkins, on the contrary, fought heroically if unsuccessfully against his own natural tendencies and reserved his erotic impulses for the only lover he had ever known, which was Christ. But this means also that the repressed energies were allowed to flow, once the dam was burst through the 'permission' to write the poem of his life.

Advising Bridges on how to read it in his letter (13 May 1878), Hopkins borrows his own metaphor: 'The *Deutschland* on her first run worked very much and unsettled you, thickening and clouding your mind with vulgar mud-bottom and common sewage (I see that I am going it with the image) . . . whereas if you had let your thoughts cast themselves . . . Why, sometimes one enjoys and admires the very lines one cannot understand . . . Besides you would have got more weathered to the style and its features – not really odd'.

Hopkins allowed poetry one moment in seven years to invade his spiritual journey and cause the most amazing shipwreck. He believed he was allowing this to happen for reasons that themselves became washed away by the storm that the poetry unleashed. The result is a poem that he humbly acknowledges as neither his own creation, nor his to change. It was taken over, as he was taken over, by another power of inspiration. The poem itself shows 'How a lush-kept plush-capped sloe/ Will, mouthed to flesh-burst,/ Gush!' The sexual imagery and movement is patent even if it were not so to Hopkins himself. The same is true for many of his lines which, read over a hundred years later, are so clearly the overflow of a repressed homoerotic sexuality that they are almost humourous, but nonetheless wonderful for that. It is when his control and his will-power were broken and he allowed the language free rein, that his genius rode the lines like riding a river. Where Hopkins allows himself to surrender to the rhythm and be drawn into the storm of his poetry, as he describes the tall nun doing in her particular stormy situation, the poems become incarnations of the Spirit, transubstantiations of flesh into word. Where he comes up for air to preach or to pray, he loses the charism of his particular ministry of the word. He is saying rather than doing his work.

The 'invention' of 'sprung rhythm' and the use of binary parallelism that characterise his mature work has been attributed by Helen Vendler, for instance, to 'a mixture of Greek and Anglo-Saxon practice' on the one hand and 'to his most fundamental intuition of the beautiful – that the beautiful was dangerous, irregular, and binary' on the other.[5] Such may indeed be the case at the literary level of proximate, secondary, efficient causation but it is a narrow myopic view of the total phenomenon. Even if we confine ourselves to strictly literary influences, we must also include the essential features of Hebrew verse, which Hopkins had studied at Oxford under the famous professor Bishop Robert Lowth, and the search for unity in diversity embodied in the thought of such pre-Socratic philosophers as Parmenides and Heraclitus.

The Hebrew sources for Hopkins mature poetry place him in a tradition of religious verse, more ancient and mystical than the narrow confines of so-called English literature, although it is also true that Hebrew verse employed the same rhythmic principle as early English verse, for which Hopkins invented the term 'sprung rhythm'.

It has been established that the use of 'parallelism' in the mature poetry of Hopkins is indebted to Hebrew poetry.[6] In fact, Hopkins has had an influence on the way the Hebrew psalms were translated into English in the twentieth century, especially in those versions used for recitation or singing.[7] This device provides a structure germane to the highly personalised intuitions of the poet, at a psychological level, but it is also an ontological principle. I would agree with Hillis-Miller's analysis of the ontological level through Hopkins' poem 'Pied Beauty'which he sees as 'a model in little of the universe it names.'[8] Beauty in this world is always pied, always in relationship with what is similar to it though never identical. Skies are dappled, cows are brinded, trout are stippled and every natural thing is 'plotted and pieced' between what is similar and what is different. Beauty is the 'copresence of the two, unlikeness with likeness, sameness with difference'. Poetry can express such beauty by revealing the relation of likeness in difference and by making these echo and chime. The ultimate version of pied beauty is God, in whom maximum diversity achieves ultimate unity.

Pied Beauty

Glory be to God for dappled things –
For skies of couple-colour as a brinded cow;
For rose-moles all in stipple upon trout that swim;
Fresh-firecoal chestnut-falls; finches' wings;
Landscape plotted and pieced – fold, fallow, and plough;
And all trades, their gear and tackle and trim.

All things counter, original, spare, strange;
Whatever is fickle, freckled (who knows how?)
With swift, slow; sweet, sour; adazzle, dim;
He fathers-forth whose beauty is past change:
Praise him.

This poem is a curtal, or abbreviated sonnet, which divides into two parts. Each part echoes, mirrors and parallels the other, in the way that God relates to the world. The poem is the language which shows how 'the creator and the creation rhyme'.

However, I say more. There is a further level, which is theological and which incorporates and subsumes both the psychological and the ontological. In this case it is the essentially Christian understanding of the Triune God, as lover rather than creator. And in the poetry here in question, the pattern is triadic, following the energy, movement and specific personhood of each member of the Trinity. It is a further intimate pattern woven between the woof and warp of the diadic, necessarily antithetical and antagonistic structure of the created universe, which itself contains that integral unity within diversity (universe) that Hopkins experienced and learned to formulate from his study of Greek philosophy. The 'more' which Hopkins added to develop his own 'inscape', that perception of the universe which he understood to be his vocation to share with the rest of us, is a deeper insight, one that reveals the sacrament, the presence of the Trinity, the triadic reality within the binary appearance. Here he is directly indebted to an intuition transmitted to him by Duns Scotus which was different from the 'creational' intuition of accepted and orthodox Thomist theology. For Thomas the essential intuition was one of participated Being: the link between the created and the uncreated which was a huge insuperable abyss spanned only by the person of Christ as a 'vinculum', a 'buckle', a bridge over the divide. The theology that Hopkins derived from Duns Scotus was more akin to the Orthodox theology of Divine energies suffusing and infiltrating, without thereby becoming absorbed in, or identified with, the 'nature' they were penetrating like fire. It was a theology of love, of energy, of transfiguration, rather than of power, of created grace, of transformation.

Even 'Pied Beauty', always quoted as the supreme example of the binary parallellism in Hopkins, is riddled with triadic pattern. The so-called 'curtal' or curtailed sonnet, actually allows the poem to be divided into a succession of threes made up of deliberately indented tercets, each one describing the Father as creator, the Son as redeemer and the Holy Ghost as Sanctifier, and within the tercets themselves to have a succession of words and phrases knitted together in clusters of three. Thus the second tercet begins 'Fresh-firecoal' (the natural raw material created by the Father which allows the sacrifice of the Son and the purifying fire of the Spirit to later emerge as 'immortal diamond'), 'chestnut-falls' (referring to the sacrifice of Christ, his 'fall', from heaven, from grace, from the cross, which redeemed ours. And these words, hyphenated to identify them as a cluster, carry the image of the seed sown for the harvest and the horse as symbol of Christ), 'finches' wings' as images of the Holy Ghost, whose 'Ah, bright wings' are recognisable references.

From this line all seems to unfold in threes: 'fold, fallow, and plough'; 'gear and tackle and trim'. Even the famous antitheses used to illustrate the parallel dyads occur in a group of three divided by semi-colons: 'swift, slow; sweet, sour; adazzle, dim;' and if what I am saying is true, and these triadic patterns are deliberate and purposeful, then it becomes clear that in the first line of the 'sestet' of this sonnet, the third word 'counter' must be a verb meaning to oppose, contradict, parry, neutralize, act as counterbalance to, allowing the last three adjectives to form a triad referring, each in turn, to the Father as 'original', the Son as 'spare' and the Holy Ghost as 'strange'.

Whether one accepts the details of this triadic structure and trinitarian pattern, and it is possible to become overly zealous in its application, once alerted to the possibility, it is ungainsayable that such a preoccupation was central to Hopkins' mind and project. Hopkins used triads of words, phrases, lines, verses, to symbolise, celebrate and, more importantly, to incarnate the reality that underpinned his own life, the inscape of the world around him, which he tried to convey in his poetry.

'Let me be to Thee as a circling bird' Hopkins asks God in a sonnet of 1865. His great fear was that love of other things might deflect him from his goal, yet again enunciated in the trinitarian triad of 'Love, O my God, to call Thee Love and Love.' In November of the same year he wrote in his journal: 'On this day by God's grace, I resolved to give up all beauty until I had his leave for it.'⁹ The following year, 1866, he became a Roman Catholic and in 1868 entered the novitiate of the Jesuit order. At this decisive moment he destroyed his own copies of his early poetry because such work seemed to him to conflict with the vocation he had now chosen.

It was in 1872 that he received the 'revelation' through his reading of the theology of Duns Scotus, which was the realisation that the beauty of God and the beauty of the world are not contrary opposites but rather participations in one another. The notion that Hopkins later called 'inscape' was essentially a mystical insight that all ontology is essentially inherent Christology, if one has the eye for the essential.

One of the theological dogmas that caused Hopkins to leave his own denomination and become a Roman Catholic, was the real presence of Christ in the Eucharist, technically referred to as transubstantiation, whereby the bread and wine on the altar become the body and blood of Christ. Duns Scotus allowed him to extend this intuition to the whole of creation. Every fragment of creation is potentially a Eucharistic element and Hopkins now saw his vocation as a priest/poet to make such sacraments available to God's people. This revelation was 'a mercy from God' who, through it, had now given Hopkins 'His leave' to both examine the beauty of the world around him and to express it. The journal entry for August 1872 which records this new discovery conveys something of his excitement and relief: 'Flush with a new stroke of enthusiasm. It may come to nothing or it may be a mercy from God. But just then when I took in any inscape of the sky or sea I thought of Scotus.'[10]

Hopkins was studying theology from 1874 to 1877, the year of his ordination to the priesthood, and during this comparatively happy time at St Beuno's in Wales,[11] he developed this merciful intuition into a highly refined understanding of the mystery of God's real presence in this world. The poems he wrote during this same year contain among them his most perfect expression of natural beauty as divinely inscribed. The poem which is most successful as an incarnation of the 'lovescape' he apprehended in the world, is 'The Windhover'. 'Here' he achieves transubstantiation through word and rhythm in a liturgy 'to Christ our Lord' of elements which present themselves as fragments of creation but which become manifestations of the Trinity.

In 'God's Grandeur' and in 'As kingfishers catch fire', where he mentions explicitly Christ and the Holy Ghost, his incarnations are not as total or as transubstantiated. These poems remain homilies in part, or sermons on the sacrament; words more than deeds. 'The world is charged with the grandeur of God.' And note how this poem about God's Grandeur becomes in the second line a hymn to the second person of the Trinity who flames out 'like shining from shook foil' in his specific role as manifestation, as light of light, as icon of the divinity, whereas the third line describes the presence of the Holy Spirit, that 'gathers to a greatness, like the ooze of oil', the traditional symbol of the third person in all forms of anointing, and in 'gathering' together and leading on to greatness, holiness, divine likeness. However, even more so, 'The Windhover' is a poetic deed, a Eucharistic sacrament, which Hopkins told Bridges was one of the best things he had ever written.

The inscape of nature which the poem 'catches' is more refined than in any previous poems. It is a Trinitarian vision with all three persons tracing the particularity of their specific charism in the movement, the imagery and the words. The sonnet form is here used, not as a diptych to stress alternation, parallellism, contrast, but as a triptych, using two tercets after the octave to develop the theme and incorporate the third person.

Writing to Dixon in 1881, Hopkins says that 'the equation of the best sonnet is $(4+4) + (3+3)$'[12] and he wrote out the poem with spaces between lines indicating such a threefold division. Also, in this poem, Hopkins banishes metaphor completely. We do not begin with 'as' or 'like'; we 'catch' the real presence: the poem is the windhover, it is what it says.

This, in sonnet form, is Hopkins' theological vision, the mystery of the Trinity, and his most perfect expression of that for which he forsook everything in his life, the Real Presence of God in our world. In a letter to Bridges he says that 'It is the true mystery, the incomprehensible one' which we cannot explain 'by grammar or by tropes' but which, for convinced Catholics, 'leaves their minds swinging; poised, but on the quiver.'[13]

Hopkins opens the poem and introduces his vision with the words 'I caught' which mean more than to catch sight of, they infer: 'I instressed, caught, "stalled" the object at the greatest intensity of pitch.'[14] In other words, this is the moment forecast in 'The Wreck of the Deutschland':

> His mystery must be instressed, stressed;
> For I greet him the days I meet him, and bless when I
>   understand.

It is also the fulfilment of that last line of his 1865 sonnet, 'Love, O my God, to call Thee Love and Love', except that here each repeated word of the trinity of love receives its proper name.

'Morning' divides the time-scheme of the poem into three parts. A later (1879) poem, 'Morning, Midday and Evening Sacrifice' is divided specifically into three verses of seven lines each. The first, addressed to God the Father, uses a vocabulary similar to the octave of 'The Windhover' (dappled/wimpled); the second is held 'at Christ's employment'; the third echoes the 'blue-bleak embers' of the final tercet of 'The Windhover', 'In silk-ash kept from cooling/And ripest under rind', both of which suggest evening and fire as emblematic of the Holy Spirit.

The triadic pattern of the poem is repeated constantly in groups of words and phrases as well as in the structure of the whole sonnet. In the second line, two sets of three words each beginning with 'd', with the second set hyphenated into a triple worded adjective, suggest the three kinds of grace which Hopkins attributed to the corresponding persons of the Trinity.

'Dapple' is the code word for the 'Pied Beauty' of creation, which is the work of that 'quickening' grace that 'belongs to God the Father'. 'Dawn' is the image regularly applied to the second person of the Trinity throughout the bible and the history of spiritual writing. The Incarnation and birth of Christ have often been compared with a light that shines in the darkness, 'the dawn from on high that breaks upon us'.[15] It is his 'purifying and mortifying grace' that is our 'redemption' or 'salvation'. Finally, 'drawn' can be applied to the Pentecostal grace of the Holy Spirit, which leads us back to the Father, draws us upwards, for His is that grace 'which lifts the receiver from one cleave of being to another and to a vital act in Christ: This is truly God's finger touching the very vein of personality, which nothing else can reach.'[16] 'Grace is any action, activity, on God's part by which, in creating or after creating, he carries the creature to or towards the end of its being, which is its self-sacrifice to God and its salvation.'[17] Grace therefore is act and as act is mostly the work of the Holy Spirit in our day, that is, after the year AD (*Anno Domini*) when the second person of the Trinity came on earth. Hopkins distinguishes between the graceful activity of each person of the Trinity in ways that correspond to the distinctions which I am suggesting here between the words and phrases of this and other poems. He calls the Father's 'creative' grace, the Son's '"medicinal," corrective, redeeming,' grace, and the Holy Ghost's 'elevating' grace.[18]

The Windhover
To Christ Our Lord

I caught this morning morning's minion, King-
    dom of daylight's daupin, dapple-dawn-drawn Falcon,
      in his riding
    Of the rolling level underneath him steady air, and striding
      striding
High there, how he rung upon the rein of a wimpling wing
In his ecstasy! then off, off forth on swing,
    As a skate's heel sweeps smooth on a bow-bend: the hurl and gliding
      the hurl and gliding
Rebuffed the big wind. My heart in hiding
Stirred for a bird, —the achieve of, the mastery of the thing!

Brute beauty and valour and act, oh, air, pride, plume here
    Buckle! AND the fire that breaks from thee then, a billion
    Times told lovlier, more dangerous, O my chevalier!

No wonder of it shéer plód makes plough down sillion
Shine, and blue-bleak embers, ah my dear,
    Fall, gall themselves, and gash gold-vermilion.

'King' in the first line of 'The Windhover' rhymes with 'wing', then with 'swing' and eventually with the last word of the octave 'thing'. This 'thing', which is also the windhover, both as 'pride' and 'plume', in its natural and its written form, is the fragment of creation which Hopkins uses as the element of his Eucharistic prayer, his trinitarian anaphora, leaving our minds 'swinging' as he 'catches' the essence of it. 'Stress is the making a thing more, or making it markedly, what it already is. It is the bringing out of its nature'.[19] Hopkins reveals the real nature of the windhover for what it already is: the real presence of the body and blood of Christ, which, in turn, is the incarnate economy of all three persons of the Trinity. God is 'King' and the windhover is king in the first line of the poem, only to be drawn down, to fall, into his kingdom in the next line. The breaking of the word reveals the essentially sacrificial nature of the King's role in His kingdom, of God's presence in our world. It parallels exactly the corresponding words, holding equivalent place, in the opening lines of the sestet: 'here/Buckle'. King becomes kingdom, that word is made flesh, through the mystery of incarnation, which is the essential role, inscape, of Christ, not just when He came on earth, but from the moment that God uttered the word-world. *Agnus qui occisus est ab origine mundi*, in the words of Revelation (13:8). And 'kingdom' became such, and became ours, through the further *kenosis*, the self-emptying fall, descent, spread-eagled collapse, of the Crucifixion on the one hand, with its concomitant fructiferousness through the Holy Spirit on the other. At the lower level, on the second line, in the economy of the kingdom itself, the king is reduced to being 'dom of daylight's dauphin'. 'Dom' in itself is an abbreviated form of the Latin 'Dominus' which is sometimes used as a title in ecclesiastical circles. It completes the set of alliterative triads describing the trinitarian economy working 'at the rolling level underneath'. The first set applies to the Trinity in its relationships within, as Father, Son and Spirit; the second triad, 'dapple-dawn-drawn' describes the Trinity 'ad extra' in relationship to the world. Both sets and all three persons are recapitulated in the 'Falcon, in his riding', and this word is both capitalised and synonymous with the windhover in the economy of the poem, even though not ornithologically exact. Its aptness 'here' is its first syllable which chimes with the developing imagery and sound of the 'fall'.

This tripartite structure, if accepted as paradigmatic, allows us to group the words immediately preceding the notorious enigma of the tenth line. What actually *does* 'Buckle' then, in such a reading, are two sets of three nouns separated by the interjection 'Oh'. The first set, 'brute beauty and valour and act' would represent three aspects of the windhover which correspond to the threefold nature of grace as energy infused by each person of the Trinity: brute beauty is the work of creation, valour is the work of redemption, and the last is the work of the Holy Spirit which as sanctification is the lifting up of the receiver 'to a vital act in Christ.'[20] The second set: 'air, pride, plume' describe these same Trinitarian energies or grace as perceived through the inscape of the windhover itself, what surrounds it in space, what gives it its 'valour', what allows it to fly.

All these sets of three, along with every convoluted triad of the sonnet, are required to 'Buckle' in both senses of the word,[21] at the appropriate moment, 'here' and now at the consecration. The word acts as a vortex. Up to 'here' every verb is in the past tense. The octave as account of creation and the history of the world culminates in the anamnesis, the remembering and representation of the ultimate moment of sacrifice when and where Christ redeemed the time. This moment is made really present, present tense, by the priest/poet, under the appearance of birdflesh. Just as the crusaders when dying on the battlefields used to reach up and consume leaves from trees which they blessed with the words of consecration, transubstantiated these fragments of creation into the body and blood of Christ, so Hopkins, under the imaginative tutelage of Duns Scotus, creates the words of consecration which can transform the windhover into the real presence of the Trinity for those who have ears to hear with. At this moment, in this verb 'breaks', the poem changes to the present tense; because after the moment celebrated here, the 'fraction', there is only present tense and time – *hodie*.

The 'thee' from whom the fire breaks is, then, both bird and Christ, because the mysterious transubstantiation has taken place: 'The Windhover' remains as bird, as text, and as Real Presence of Christ which perdures. It is a mystical vision which becomes available to the reader through the techniques of the poetry and the contemplative capacity of the beholder. 'My heart in hiding/ Stirred for a bird, – the achieve of, the mastery of the thing!' The poem is the ingenius mediator between the inscape of the 'thing' and 'instress' in the reader. The 'haeceitas' of the particular falcon is revealed in all its glory by the achievement of the poem. 'A bird' is X-rayed through to its sacramental propensity to represent the real presence of the Trinity:[22]

> Suppose God showed us in a vision the whole world enclosed first in a drop of water, allowing everything to be seen in its native colours; then the same in a drop of Christ's blood, by which everything whatever was turned scarlet, keeping nevertheless mounted in the scarlet its own colour too.

'The Windhover' articulates just such a vision except that 'here' the whole world is enclosed in the windhover itself, as a particular bird, 'seen in all its native colours'. Then 'the same' is

seen in 'a drop of Christ's blood', as 'gold-vermilion'. The work
of the Holy Spirit is to achieve the conjunction, the hypenation
of what I am and what Christ is, without spilling a drop of the
native colour of either.

The famous 'enormous' conjunction, if also divided into its
three component parts, suggests in cypher form the same
chronological revolution which AD has formulated in the
history of the world. It represents a new age, a new time, the
inauguration of the time of resurrection. This new age, new
time, is always present, but it can only be re-enacted by the
power of the Holy Spirit, the third person of the Trinity. The
first person created the wherewithal, the second person
initiated the possibility, the third person multiplies that original
act by making it available at all times and everywhere, making
Christ play 'in ten thousand places, . . . to the Father through
the features of men's faces.'

In other words, returning to the enormous and capitalised
conjunction, we can say that it is the Holy Spirit who raises the
AD of that conjunction to the Nth degree, to the power of N, 'a
billion/Times told lovelier' through the Eucharistic mystery.
The 'AND' therefore has the position and the force of an
epiclesis in the technical terminology of liturgical theology, an
invocation of the Holy Spirit to transform the offering into the
Body and Blood of Christ for the spiritual nourishment of
those who receive these. As a conjunction it has the power of
such formulae as the 'filioque' which attempted to describe in
a three-letter paratactical adjunct the way in which the grace of
the Holy Spirit conjoins with the grace of Christ to effect 'the
fire that breaks from thee then', and succeeded only in dividing
Christendom into irreconcilable factions. This 'AND' of
Hopkins is THE conjunction expressing the whole trinitarian
economy of salvation at the exact moment of enactment,
when a permanent conjunction was grafted like a hyphen

between humanity and divinity, achieving the ultimate 'Pied Beauty'. It is the mysterious conjunction made possible by the 'Fall' of the Son.

The Holy Spirit, who presides over the final tercet of the poem, as The Holy Spirt does also over 'Nature as a Heraclitean Fire', to work it towards resurrection as Immortal Diamond, mounts in scarlet and 'gold-vermilion' the 'shéer plód' of our daily lives, precisely because of that conjunction which links us, here and now, to the ever-present tense of Christ's sacrificial act.

The triadic pattern which permeates the poem and moves towards a central vortex, mirrors the presence of the Trinity in all of creation and in every fragment of creation, like a watermark at 'the rolling level underneath' and allows Hopkins to achieve a synthesis of threes that haunted him. Nor is it just the Trinity of divine persons that are made word in this poem; there is also the elemental world of air, water, earth, which are consumed and transformed by the 'fire that breaks from thee then'; God, the windhover and the poet are also 'dapple-dawn-drawn' into linguistic conjunction, through that other recalcitrant triad of: words, world, and we ourselves.

In a sermon of 1888, Hopkins tells us that:

> St Ignatius speaks of the angel discharging his mission, it being question of action leading up to, as now my action leads from, the Incarnation. The Incarnation was for my salvation and that of the world: the work goes on in a great system and machinery which even drags me on with the collar around my neck.

This quotation describes also the work of this poem in which Hopkins discharges his mission. His sonnet is not 'about' the windhover, it is the windhover. At no moment does he interject his homiletic tendency or pedagogy. His heart remains in hiding. He elaborates 'a great system and machinery' to 'catch' the bird and transubstantiate it into the real presence of the one to whom the poem is dedicated. Hopkins knew that AD had rendered metaphor anachronistic. The word must be made flesh. The word must be and not be about. This poem also achieves seamless unity between poet, language and thing. The poet is incarnate in the poem, not aloof, explaining or preaching. Everything in him and the inscape of the bird 'flush and fuse the language'.[23]

> God's utterance of himself in himself is God the Word, outside himself is this world. This world then is word, expression, news of God. Therefore its end, its purpose, its purport, its meaning, is God and its life or work to name and praise him.

Hopkins' language is strange and his poetry is difficult because it is theological vision put into words. He knew that this was what his vocation was and what his language was for. He wrote, almost obstinately to Bridges (1 April 1885): 'If you do not like it [my music] it is because there is something you have not seen and I see. That at least is my mind, and if the whole world agreed to condemn it or see nothing in it I should only tell them to take a generation and come to me again'. It is interesting to note that a hundred years later Von Balthasar's theological appraisal of his music is translated into English. And the vision which he portrays is of the world as a crucifix where God as lover of humankind prepares us for what we really are, what we really should be, his equals in love. So, the world is a shipwreck where we are brought beyond ourselves, forced to transcend the workaday world, shaken out of our mortal skins. There were two shipwrecks in Hopkins' own spiritual life: the first was that smug little world of the Jesuit novitiate where he renounced everything and watched himself like a prisoner in solitary confinement, holding his breath until he would pass into the next world without spot, stain, or wrinkle. 'The Wreck of the Deutschland' washed out that little world and the flood of language swept him into a vaster vision.

Thomas Merton, who in some ways had a temperament and a spiritual journey somewhat similar to Hopkins, makes an interesting observation:[24]

> Hopkins' spiritual struggles fought their way out in problems of rhythm. He made his asceticism bearable by thrusting it over into the order of art where he could handle it more objectively.

The second great shipwreck in his life was expressed in the terrible sonnets 'wrung from him almost unbidden' where his style is so sparse and his diction so minimally plain, that his art itself is shipwrecked and he is 'pitched past pitch of grief' where he goes beyond himself, beyond his art and beyond despair.

The last great sonnet he wrote (dated July 26 1888) is describing the whole universe and nature itself as a natural disaster area in which the individual human person is mouthed to perfection by a voraciously loving God. The Resurrection is described as a beacon of light which 'Across my foundering deck shone.' So, once again we are in the context of the shipwreck as 'the sacrament of the world'. But this more extravagant sacrifice is better imaged in the element of fire rather than water. Hopkins sees each one of us being purified and prepared for everlasting life as nature burns up all its surface matter and eventually, through various processes of purification by fire, as in a potter's kiln, the diamond that is each one of us at our deepest and our best, is formed. And as immortal diamond we are as Christ is, because we have been transubstantiated into his flesh and blood, the most perfect and most peculiarly personal version of our own.

> In a flash, at a trumpet crash,
> I am all at once what Christ is, since he was what I am,
> and
> This Jack, joke, poor potsherd, patch, matchwood,
>   immortal diamond,
> Is immortal diamond.

Notes

1   Norman White quotes this view from a letter he received from William Sargant, an eminent psychiatrist, in his book *Gerard Manley Hopkins in Wales* (London, 1998), p. 150.

2   All letters of Hopkins to Dixon are quoted from the volume produced by C.C. Abbott, *The Correspondence of Gerard Manley Hopkins to R.W. Dixon*, 2nd edn, revised (London, 1955, repr. 1970) and those of Hopkins to Robert Bridges from *The Letters of Gerard Manley Hopkins to Robert Bridges*, ed. by C.C. Abbott, 2nd edn, revised (London, 1955, repr. 1970).

3   All references to the journals of Hopkins are taken from *The Journals and Papers of Gerard Manley Hopkins*, ed. Humphrey House and Graham Storey, (London, 1959).

4   Hans Urs von Balthasar, *The Glory of the Lord, A Theological Aesthetics Vol III: Studies in Theological styles* (Edinburgh, T&T Clark, 1986), p. 387.

5   Helen Vendler, *The Breaking of Style* (HUP, 1995), pp. 9-10.

6   'Hopkins continually turned to parallelism as his point of departure for discussing poetry . . . In light of these essays, we must come to see chiming, alliteration, assonance, and sprung rhythm as aspects of a larger, more inclusive phenomenon, the phenomenon of parallelism.' Maria R. Lichtmann, *The Contemplative Poetry of Gerard Manley Hopkins* (Princeton U.P., 1989), p. 7.

7   'Hebrew verse was organised on an accentual basis. Every line had a stipulated number of accented or stressed syllables, although the total number of syllables in the line was variable. In this respect

Hebrew verse employed the same rhythmic principle as early English verse, for which Gerard Manley Hopkins invented the term "sprung rhythm". Sprung rhythm, as Hopkins observed, is to be found also in much of our later poetry and frequently occurs in nursery rhymes and popular jingles. A simple instance is to be found in 'Three blind mice'. Each line has 3 stressed syllables and a fourth beat. But the number of syllables in the line varies between 3 and 11. That all the lines may be sung simultaneously shows that they all have the same rhythmic structure of 4 beats.' *The Psalms, A New Translation from the Hebrew arranged for singing to the Psalmody of Joseph Gelineau.* (Fontana, 1966), p. 11.

8   J. Hillis-Miller, *The Disappearance of God* (HUP, 1963), pp. 298-305.

9   op. cit., House and Storey, p. 71.

10   ibid., p. 221.

11   Described by Norman White in *Gerard Manley Hopkins in Wales,* op. cit.

12   *The Correspondence of Gerard Manley Hopkins and R.W. Dixon,* op. cit., pp. 71-2.

13   *The Letters of Gerard Manley Hopkins to Robert Bridges,* op. cit., pp. 186-8. Letter of 24 October 1883.

14   Virginia Ridley Ellis, *Gerard Manley Hopkins and the Language of Mystery* (University of Missouri Press, 1991), p. 199, and also, as advised by this author, House and Storey, op.cit, pp. 221, 227, 241-2.

15   The Benedictus canticle of Zechariah (Luke: 1, 78) which Hopkins would have recited every day of his life as a Jesuit at the Office of Lauds.

16   *The Sermons and Devotional Writings of Gerard Manley Hopkins,* ed. by Christopher Devlin SJ (London, OUP, 1959), p. 327.

17   ibid., p. 154.

18   ibid., p. 158.

19   *The Further Letters of Gerard Manley Hopkins,* ed. by C.C. Abbott, 2nd edn (London, OUP, 1956), p. 327. Letter of 7 November 1883.

20   Devlin, op. cit., p. 158.

21   I agree with Maria R. Lichtmann that 'both of the most proffered interpretations of 'Buckle!' – as 'connection' and as 'collapse' – are right . . .' op. cit. note 4 above, p. 119.

22   Devlin, op. cit., p. 194.

23   Ibid., p. 129.

24   Thomas Merton, *The Sign of Jonas* (London, 1953), p. 79.

CHAPTER SIX

Christianity and the Irish

THE PURPOSE OF this book is, as far as possible, to persuade the Irish people of the twenty-first century not to abandon a very deep and ingrained devotion to Christianity and to the Eucharist. The fact that most of our population has become highly educated should mean, not that we abandon our dearest and deepest practices but that we should try to understand them more fully, although understanding is not necessary to their implementation or their survival.

The book is the third of a trilogy. What has been argued previously need not be repeated although it might be borne in mind as prelude to what is being offered here. None of it is necessary for understanding what I write here. Each book is an independent argument even though each one connects with the other as the past and the present connect with the future. Here I am talking about our future. Whatever kind of society emerges in Ireland in this new century will not be comprehensively adequate if it excludes any dimension of our humanity, or if it is narrower than both God and the whole of humankind.

The title of the book is borrowed from the image used in one of Seamus Heaney's poems and quoted by him when he was receiving the Nobel Prize for literature in 1995.[1]

The annals say: when the monks of Clonmacnoise
Were all at prayers inside the oratory
A ship appeared above them in the air.

The anchor dragged along behind so deep
It hooked itself into the altar rails
And then, as the big hull rocked to a standstill,

A crewman shinned and grappled down the rope
And struggled to release it. But in vain.
'This man can't bear our life here and will drown,'

The abbot said, 'unless we help him.' So
They did, the freed ship sailed, and the man climbed back
Out of the marvellous as he had known it.

The poet here, in his own words, is struggling with
'contradictory allegiances . . . to the numinous and to the
matter-of-fact', two dimensions which must receive equal
attention if our passage to the future is to be rooted and on
course. All the success in the world will be sawdust and tinsel
unless our connection with the depths of our own reality and
the reality of the marvellous is maintained. The purpose of this
book is to suggest how this can be done and the role which, as
always in Ireland, both monks and artists can and must play, and
the connection which should exist between them.

'On you go now! Run, son, like the devil
And tell your mother to try
To find me a bubble for the spirit level

Monasteries can act as just such bubbles for the Spirit level and
the poet here, with his ever-present humour, is sent on a quest

to find such a place. This is the place 'beyond' our 'psychic space' and one that is unattainable unless 'I thought of walking round and round a space / utterly empty, utterly a source / . . . Silent, beyond silence listened for'.

Heaney has been there. His poetry speaks from there.

> Then I entered a strongroom of vocabulary
> Where words like urns that had come through the fire
> Stood in their bone-dry alcoves next a kiln
>
> And came away changed, like the guard who'd seen
> The stone move in a diamond-blaze of air
> Or the gates of horn behind the gates of clay.

Liturgy holds like a strongroom the vocabulary of worship, where rites and words, elements and actions have come through the fire of testing through history and now stand in their bone-dry alcoves like the dry bones which Ezechiel beheld in the valley where the Spirit had led him, a valley full of bones (Ezechiel 37:1–14).

> He said to me, 'Son of man, can these bones live?' I said, 'You know, O Lord'. He said, 'Prophesy over these bones. Say, "Dry bones, hear the word of the Lord. The Lord says this to these bones: I am now going to make the breath enter you, and you will live. I shall put sinews on you, I shall make flesh grow on you, I shall cover you with skin and give you breath, and you will live; and you will learn that I am the Lord."' I prophesied as I had been ordered. While I was prophesying, there was a noise, a sound of clattering; and the bones joined together. I looked and saw that they were covered with sinews; flesh was growing on them and skin was covering them, but

there was no breath in them. He said to me, 'prophesy to the breath. Say to the breath, "The Lord says this: come from the four winds, breath; breathe on these dead; let them live!"' I prophesied as he had ordered me, and the breath entered them; they came to life again and stood on their feet, an immense army.

Then he said, 'Son of man, these bones are the whole House of Israel. They keep saying, "Our bones are dried up, our hope has gone; we are as good as dead". So prophesy. Say to them, "The Lord God says this: I am now going to open your graves; I mean to raise you from your graves, my people, and I shall put my spirit in you, and you will live, and I shall resettle you on your own soil."'

There are two 'ministers' involved in such rehabilitation and relocation of the bones of the liturgy. They are the artists and the prophets. The artists provide the sinews and the flesh, the elements of transfiguration. The prophets or the monks are what Ezechiel calls the sentinels or sentries – 'The people of the country select one of themselves and post this person as a sentry'. This person's job is to sound a horn to alert the people when anything strange or dangerous is near. 'I have appointed you as sentry. When you hear a word from my mouth, warn them in my name.'

The work of the artist is another thing. And what is 'It' or 'the Thing' that the poetry is saying? ' The Thing is a kind of 'locus', it is the focus of the 'gathering' forces of the Symbolic in its effort to domesticate the Real: 'the thing that nearly broke you'. Heaney refers to it in his Nobel speech, 'Crediting Poetry', which recalls an earlier poem, 'Fosterling':

Heaviness of being. And poetry
Sluggish in the doldrums of what happens.

Me waiting until I was nearly fifty
To credit marvels.

About the Clonmacnoise space-ship story he says: 'I take it to be pure story. It has the entrancement of a narrative that's mysterious and absolute. It needs no explanation but even so, you could read it as a text about the necessity of being in two places at the one time, on the ground with the fatherly earthiness, but also keeping your mind open and being able to go up with the kite, on the magic carpet too, and live in the world of fantasy. To live in either world entirely and resolutely, and not to shift, is risky. For your wholeness you need to inhabit both worlds. I think the medieval notion of human beings occupying the angelic situation between the angels and the beasts is true. When I wrote *Seeing Things*, I think I had been quite close to the ground, and that then I lifted up my eyes to the hills, to the roof and to the Clonmacnoise boat.'

Another poem of Seamus Heaney called 'The Forge' also describes the way in which we can hope to approach the door into the dark of the future. Somewhere near the centre of this forge there is an anvil which he desribes as an altar, 'set there immoveable' on which real iron can be beaten out and the shape and music of the future can be sketched. If we are to establish the future which will be able to house us adequately we too have to find such an altar. Forging the future requires the right kind of relationship with the true Spirit of the living God. Without this the future will be a shortsighted and inadequate plan. Relationship with this God means taking seriously the revelation of his presence and making that presence real in our workaday world.

Anchoring the altar where we pay homage to the most important elements of our lives requires, in the twenty-first century, a number of strategically placed guy-ropes and tent-pegs both to secure the edifice from dislodgement and to encourage the people to participate.

The first thing we have to state quite clearly is that what we are involved in here is a mystery and, to the best of our ability, sketch the parameters of what that means because it is not possible to explain it in logical discourse. In fact, mystery has its own way of teaching us about itself. Mystagogical was the word used by the early Christians to describe the pedagogy involved in simply attending the mysteries themselves.

Nowadays, people want to label everything, want to reduce whatever they are doing to a formula or manifesto. Many such political broadcasters tell us that the liturgy is a meal; others that it is a sacrifice; others that it is an assembly of the community; others that it is the visible enactment of the heavenly liturgy, the corporeal expression of the mystical body; others see it as thanksgiving; others as empowerment. All of these are true in certain ways, none of them are either exhaustive or exclusive. Liturgy is not reducible to any ideology, any particular version, any theology. Liturgy is *sui generis* and like the heart, has its reasons that our reason knows not of.

Wherever Christianity takes root the liturgy may take a different shape and form. 'Do this in memory of me' should be able to adapt itself to whatever culture or local surroundings require it to be done. The hymn to the Philippians (2:6–11) should apply to every aspect of Christ's life and ministry. So, although the Last Supper took a Jewish form, he did not regard this as something to be exploited, but this should empty itself to take on the form of whatever culture it is destined to serve, taking the form of a slave even, and humbling itself to that point zero where the seed must die in order to bear fruit in whatever locality or cultural environment it chooses to fall.

But here again the four presences are required to ensure that the form it takes is the genuinely local form of the designated culture. Those who know about this culture and are able to understand its length and breadth, its height and depth, who are the artists of every different kind in that country or locality, must ensure that the dynamic equivalence is maintained when the actions are translated into the milieu where they are now performed, in the same Spirit in which they were originated. Inculturation should assume all the principles and attitudes of its original model, incarnation.

Taking bread and wine meant taking whatever are the most normal foodstuffs of the area. To insist that wine of the grape be used in countries where it is never produced or used is obtuseness to the point of caricature; a caricature already lambasted by Christ himself on so many occasions throughout the Gospels. 'Alas for you, scribes and Pharisees, you hypocrites! You who clean the outside of cup and dish and leave the inside full of extortion and intemperance' (Matthew 23:25). 'They tie up heavy burdens and lay them on your shoulders, but will they lift a finger to move them? Not they!' (Ibid 23:4) 'Hypocrites! It was you Isaiah meant when he so rightly prophesied:

> This people honours me only with lip-service,
> While their hearts are far from me.
> The worship they offer me is worthless;
> The doctrines they teach are only human regulations.'

And when the disciples told him that the Pharisees were shocked at what he said 'He called the people to him and said, "Listen, and understand. What goes into a person's mouth does not make them unclean; it is what comes out of the mouth that makes you unclean."' Or when the Pharisees noticed that his disciples were picking ears of corn and eating them on the sabbath and reprimanded him, Jesus replied: 'Have you not read that what David did when he and his followers were hungry – how he went into the house of God and how they ate the loaves of offering which neither he nor his followers were allowed to eat, but which were for the priests alone? . . . For the Son of Man is master of the sabbath' (Matt 12: 1–8).

'Give us this day our daily bread', not some rarefied facsimile which an age of fastidious body haters created as the nearest thing to 'spiritual' bread – *panis angelicus* – the last layer of materiality between being and nothingness. What we call 'the host' was bread with as much elemental material kneaded and pounded out of it as possible. The job of transubstantiation was being made easier by having all the natural substance pounded out so that the element becomes a see-through transparency available for radiation from the other world. The less like us and what we are and what we need and what we eat, the more sacred, holy, celestial and divine. Whether this was an expression of the Eucharist valid for the time in which it was instigated is a question for history. However, to have such an alien and arcane insight imposed upon every Eucharistic celebration in the twentieth century was deadening. Jesus said to them, 'Keep your eyes open, and be on your guard against the yeast of the Pharisees and Sadducees' (Matt 16:6).

When the dew lifted on the people of Israel who were starving in the desert they saw 'a thing, delicate, powdery, as fine as hoarfrost' on the ground and they said to one another 'What is that?' 'That,' said Moses, 'is the bread the Lord gives you to eat!' They were puzzled. They called it Manna which means 'What is that?' It was like coriander seed, white in colour and resembled wafers made with honey. Most commentators agree that these miracles in the desert were 'natural' events. The quails which arrived in abundance out of the blue were migrating across the desert from North Africa to southern Europe. Manna was most probably a secretion from insects that are found in tamarisk trees. The people of Israel were told to eat only what they needed for each day. If they hoarded any of it or kept it for the next day in their tents or tabernacles it deteriorated or bred maggots. Except for the Sabbath day when they could gather up a double portion on the day before which would last and not deteriorate. Several hundred years later they understood what had happened and they wrote in the book of Wisdom (16:20-21): 'You gave them the food of angels, from heaven untiringly sending them bread already prepared, containing every delight, satisfying every taste. And the substance you gave demonstrated your tenderness towards your children, for, conforming to the taste of whoever ate it, it transformed itself into what each eater wished'.

Every culture has its own substance, its own taste. The body and blood of the Lord was meant to be transformed into whatever is the equivalent of 'bread and wine' in yours and mine, whatever natural elements we use to nourish our bodies and quench our thirst. To impose upon other cultures and other nations the particular elements which are natural to the particular locality where Jesus Christ pitched his tent in the desert is perverse. It contradicts the liberality and generosity of the incarnation and locks up the cornucopia of God's goodness in an inaccessible storehouse to which we as guardians of the European empire hold the keys.

New wineskins for new wine! Christianity was never intended to become slavish imitation of anything or anyone. It is the opposite: every Christian as a person is as individual and unrepeatable as their finger-print. Even the Imitation of Christ is an ambiguous, even dangerous spirituality because, as Kierkegaard says, when I reach the next life I won't be asked why I was not more like Christ, I will be asked why I was not more like myself. Art is the opposite of imitation. Art that imitates is dead, is kitsch. Art is originality in both senses of the word. It springs from the source, our origins, and it expresses itself as what has never been seen or done before, as originality.

And this is what Religion needs in order to appropriate in our world its resurrectional character, to rise from the dead, to give life to its bones, to come out of an empty tomb. And the constant danger for religion is to set guards in front of the sealed door of the tomb containing the dead body of the Lord, in case anyone might come and steal him away, or in case something miraculous might happen.

And in Ireland in the twenty-first century where art is thriving and where people still believe, there is a possible meeting-place for art and Christianity that would deliver forms of worship to a world now wandering through a spiritual desert. It happened in Byzantium in the sixth century, it happened in Rome in the sixteenth century, but there is no point in resurrecting either or both those movements or those times in some attempt to reproduce the icons or the madonnas of yesteryear. The challenge and the miracle of continuing tradition is to find the forms, the materials, the elements, the substances which can give life and shape to the Spirit in our own day.

Notes

1   Seamus Heaney, *Opened Ground, Poems 1966–1996* (London, Faber & Faber, 1998), p. 364.